Poems and Paintings of Herefordshire

and the neighbouring Marches

Brian Hatton,
*Cloudy Day
at Warham*,
1911
(Hereford
Art Gallery)

Poems and Paintings of Herefordshire

and the neighbouring Marches

selected by Jonathan Lumby

Logaston Press

Brian Hatton,
*Study Towards
the Malverns*,
1885
(Hereford
Art Gallery)

David Jones,
*Landscape
at Capel-y-ffin*,
1925/6
(Monnow
Valley Arts)

LOGASTON PRESS
Little Logaston Woonton Almeley
Herefordshire HR3 6QH
www.logastonpress.co.uk

First published by Logaston Press 2017
Selection and introduction © Jonathan Lumby 2017
Copyright of poems and paintings as per pages 141-2

ISBN 978 1 910839 22 5

Typeset by Logaston Press
and printed and bound in Poland by
www.lfbookservices.co.uk

Published with the
generous support of a grant from
the Geoffrey Walter Smith Fund of the
Woolhope Naturalists' Field Club.

Contents

J.M.W. Turner,
*View of
Hampton Court
Herefordshire
from the
Northwest*
(Yale Center
for British Art)

v

John Scarlett
Davis,
*Market Hall,
Leominster,*
1820
(when the artist
was about 16)
(Hereford
Art Gallery)

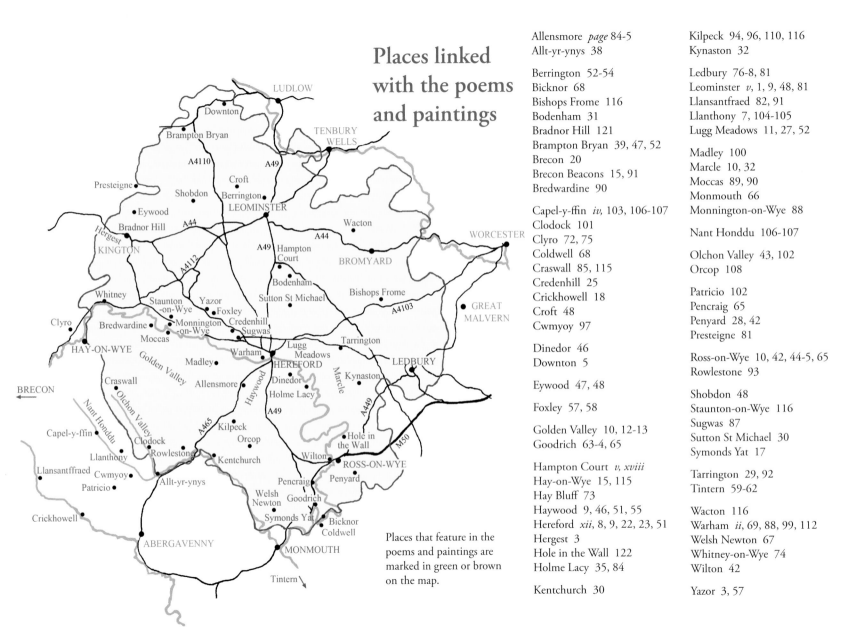

Places linked with the poems and paintings

Places that feature in the poems and paintings are marked in green or brown on the map.

Acknowledgements

I thank Alan Bailey, companion in my proof-reading, and
Philip Weaver, who has been a shaper of this book. Sue
Locke included me in a poetry-reading group. Dean Michael
Tavinor told me of *A Herefordshire Winter* and accompanied
soprano Lucy Bowen as she performed William Boyce's song.
Edward Harley generously unearthed his family's manuscript
of *The Five Sisters*. James Atherton, singer and organ-builder,
discussed the call of a cuckoo. The Traherne Association
has enlivened and inspired me, particularly its Chairman,
Richard Willmott, and its Secretary, Hilary Rosenkiewicz.
Andy and Karen Johnson, proprietors of Logaston Press,
have over decades enhanced our knowledge of Hereford's
history. Catherine Willson, director of Fine Arts at Hereford
Art Gallery, allowed me to see the wonderful work of Brian
Hatton and of other artists, and has so freely supplied
images for this book that its publication is possible. The
Woolhope Club's generous grant has allowed us to include
more works than would otherwise have been feasible.
Through kind Esther de Waal I enjoyed meeting the poets
Bonnie Thurston and Ruth Bidgood and learned of further
poets of the borderlands. Jane, my wife, poet and painter,
has been perfect as a helpmeet. Copies of this book to each
are my gift of devotion and gratitude.

Jonathan Lumby

Brian Hatton,
Elm Trees,
c.1908
(Hereford
Art Gallery)

List of poems

List of paintings

x

xii

David Cox, *Butcher's Row, Hereford*, 1815
(Hereford Art Gallery)

Introduction

Through poetry we are pitched into closeness with those of centuries past. Enjoy this garland of poems and songs. They chose me, for each poem has become 'a joy for ever', and each, besides its grace of expression, shows how people, perhaps long ago, have responded to the landscape that now we tread.

Here are paintings – watercolours from the Golden Age of Watercolour, and oil paintings. You'll see here the River Wye, the River Usk and the River Lugg, their water-meadows and their cliffs, and you'll peep at harvesters on Coppet Hill and Dinedor. There's an etching of the Great Oak of Moccas, and one of trees near Downton Castle. Gainsborough sketched a beech in Yazor.

Places in which to linger
The poems give glimpses of the history of Herefordshire and its Borderland. They tell of places graced by the attention of poets. You may like to visit these 'shrines' and to linger there.

You might go to the Golden Valley where Rowland Vaughan, praised by John Davies, wished to establish a communitarian paradise; or to Brinsop where William Wordsworth stayed with his in-laws; or to the castle-grounds of Goodrich where the poet met the maid who insisted 'We are Seven'.

In the churchyard at Orcop a stone marks the grave of Frances Horovitz – her fellow-poet Anne Stevenson on finding it wrote tenderly of her loveliness. Alexander Pope lauded the leading inhabitant of Ross-on-Wye, a wonder of civic charity.

Go, perhaps, to Credenhill, or to fields nearby where Thomas Traherne, when a child, saw the corn as 'orient and immortal wheat', and the green trees as 'strange and wonderful things'. Visit Henry Vaughan's tombstone at Llansantffraed – 'above the voiceful windings of a river'; or Patricio, undisturbed, and its holy spring. Call at Kilpeck, Clodock, Craswall or Llanthony, or see one of Herefordshire's 'unpretentious' churches 'that seem/ to rise from the earth/ as naturally as hedgerows'. Find Hergest and Yazor, homes of Chaucer's knightly friend, Sir John Clanvowe; or Brampton Bryan, seat of Robert Harley, eminent both as scholar and statesman.

The poems allude to landscape and evoke history; so this book, with maps ancient and modern, could serve as a *vade mecum* – a companion as you ramble and journey.

Sing cuccu!

The song of the cuckoo flutes through Herefordshire's poetry. As you may know, the upper note of a cuckoo's call is *E flat*, the lower most frequently *C natural*, so they form something between a minor and a major descending third.

"*Cuckoo. . . cuckoo. . . cuckoo. . .*" wrote Ronald Johnson while walking the Wye in April 1976, adding: "*I had been listening for the first cuckoo, Delius' cuckoo – / but the sound is softer, more penetrant. 'Calling / about the hills,' Kilvert says. Yes, / it is that. An echo . . .*"

The round '*Sing cuccu*' has words as early as any poem in English. In Leominster Priory in about 1275 this lyric of early summer may well first have been sung. If with friends you would sing the *rota*, you will see on the score that where every new voice enters, William of Wycombe has inscribed a red Maltese cross.

O sylvan Wye, thou wanderer

The Wye also winds through these poems and paintings, as it does through the bowl of the county. Michael Drayton rejoiced in the river which "*Oft windeth on her way, as back she meant to go./ Meander, who is said so intricate to be, / Hath not so many turns, nor crankling nooks as she.*"

On 13 July 1798 William Wordsworth paused above the Wye, observant and listening: "*again I hear/ These waters, rolling from their mountain-springs / With a soft inland murmur.*" The harmony of that wooded scene led him to contemplate profoundly, his mood becoming one in which, should we share it, "*we are laid asleep / In body, and become a living soul.*" He lavished gratitude on Herefordshire's river: "*How oft, in spirit, have I turned to thee, / O sylvan Wye. Thou wanderer thro' the woods! / How oft has my spirit turned to thee.*"

Beside the Wye, from Hay, Anne Stevenson walked early in a dazzle of sunlight.

At Hole in the Wall, where the river flows in great beauty, Margot Miller desperately feared for the safety of Dusty, her daughter, who was swimming in "*the great Welsh flood. . . ., Great Grandma Gwy*", who cajoled: "*Come to me,* Dewch i mi*, Dusty,* tirion */ I'll take you down, down where I curve and bend.*"

In 1811 Robert Bloomfield with companions boated down the Wye beyond Symonds Yat and Goodrich. In verse of lucid joy he described the landscape of the picturesque. Ronald Johnson, much later, walked upstream: "*O wind your waters through these songs, & mine – / River Wye, / green Wye.*"

Vaughan and Traherne

Two wise religious poets lived in the territory we cover: Henry Vaughan the Silurist, of the valley of the River Usk, and Thomas Traherne, child in Hereford, Rector in Credenhill. Vaughan attended Oxford in the early 1640s, Traherne in the 1650s.

We do not know whether Henry Vaughan, physician and high-Anglican scholar, ever met Thomas Traherne, the country parson, yet Vaughan and Traherne shared a belief at odds with their contemporaries. Though at that time churchmen, both Catholics and Calvinists insisted on Original Sin, our two poets held that new-born infants enter this world in glorious innocence. The mood of each is light because infused by 'Original Goodness'. Each savoured the created world. Each was unobsessed about penitence and salvation. They were joyful, loving and humble. You can see how each poet sought to recapture childhood's blissful vision. Vaughan wrote: *"Happy those early days! when I / Shin'd in my Angell-infancy . . ."*, while Thomas Traherne remembers an infancy in which *"eternity was manifest in all things"*. Precious words!

By the Wye Wordsworth assessed his more youthful days. Later, in *'Intimations of Immortality . . .'* he would say of the new-born: *"Not in entire forgetfulness, / and not in utter nakedness, / But trailing clouds of glory do we come / From God, who is our home: / Heaven lies about us in our infancy!"*

Francis Kilvert in Clyro asked a child: *"Whence do you come?"* Her reply pleased him: *"'From Paradise,' she said, and smiled."*

Is it by chance that poets in our region share an insight that was, in their day, unusual and deplored? Does the harmony of the Usk and of the Wye dispose us to embrace a 'Silurian spirituality', humane, trusting, sometimes ecstatic?

Siluria

At one time poets called Herefordshire and the nearby Marches 'Siluria'. This anthology is about Siluria.

The home of Henry Vaughan the Silurist is the most far-flung. Yet as a writer he deliberately added 'The Silurist' to his name. By this he signified that the Borderlands and Herefordshire were his *patria*, his homeland of the spirit. He had his reasons. He looked back from Wales to his grandfather's early home in Herefordshire – to the Vaughans' Bredwardine Castle by the Wye – and to his own schooling in Llangattock, closer to the border; he wrote not in Welsh but in English and in Latin; and he held fast to the faith of the English Church. By calling himself 'the Silurist' Henry Vaughan merits a hearing in a Silurian anthology.

You'll find that 'Silurian' often means 'of Herefordshire'. John Philips called apples *"Silurian Plants"*; he extolled *"Silurian Cyder"*. William Diaper called Philips one *"who once Silurian Plains adorn'd"*. John Dyer praised *"pleasant Siluria, land of various views, / Hills, rivers, woods, and lawns, and purple groves / Pomaceous . . ."*, and added a footnote: *"Siluria, the part of England which lies west of the Severn, viz. Herefordshire, Monmouthshire, &c."*

To these poets of the 1600s and early 1700s, 'Siluria' is almost 'Arcadia', a rural idyllic region. So too it was to Joshua Cristall; near his home in Goodrich, he painted Arcadian landscapes and charming harvesters.

Siluria is the land of this book. We travel from Herefordshire down the Wye and up the Usk. We extend over Hatterall Hill and the Black Mountains. The poems shape these borders. They express a culture.

Welshness in the soil's depth

The poems raise the question: is Herefordshire, deep down in its spirit, in England or in Wales?

Michael Drayton, in his geography-in-verse, grouped Herefordshire alongside the counties of south-east Wales, thus helping "*to uphold*", he explained, "*the ancient bounds of Wales, the Severne, and Dee*" and to restore the county to its "*ancient mother, Wales*". John Davies of Hereford called Rowland Vaughan (Henry's kinsman) "*Glory of Wales*", though Rowland had been born in Bredwardine and was active in the Golden Valley. Our contemporary, Ruth Bidgood, discerns in Clodock (or Clydawg) "*a place of shifting boundaries*" wherein is "*Welshness in the soil's depth*".

Of course, since mediaeval times and earlier, the valleys of the Dore and the Monnow especially have shifted in language, diocese, lordship and culture. English-Welsh boundaries here have remained porous; this is a theme of the writer Esther de Waal (Moir), about whom we must say more.

Hospitality to poets

As well as poets some others merit a place in the story of Silurian poetry.

Brampton Bryan's Robert Harley, Earl of Oxford and First Minister in Queen Anne's reign, was a man of learned and literary bent who chose to be generous to John Philips, poet of *Cyder*, and was friend to Alexander Pope. Pope dined too with Lady Frances Scudamore of Holme Lacy, widow of the 3rd Viscount, patronesss to John Gay and his literary circle, and with the great Jacob Tonson, his London publisher, by then retired to an estate in Ledbury. At their tables Pope learned about 'The Man of Ross'.

The Vaughan Association was founded by poets meeting in 1996 to celebrate Henry Vaughan's tercentenary. Each year it holds a friendly poetic colloquy in the Usk Valley, and publishes *Scintilla: a journal of literary criticism,* through which it promotes new writing broadly in the spirit of Henry Vaughan. Anne Cluysenaar was the Association's lively Secretary, Peter Thomas its Chairman, and Ruth Bidgood and Esther de Waal are among its members.

Anne Cluyesnaar visited Esther de Waal's cottage garden in Rowlestone. In merriment she exclaimed: "*She's up that old plum tree, bare-footed, / pitchfork in hand ...*" Esther was gathering fruit, and by quiet attraction she has also gathered poets. Frances Horovitz and Roger Garfitt, living in the Mill below her cottage, dedicated 'Rowlestone Haiku' to Esther, her sister and their families. Later they lived not far away. Bonnie Thurston comes from the US to visit the border country – her poems were published following discussion around Esther's kitchen table; Ruth Bidgood is a dear friend to Esther, and both to Bonnie; and Anne Stevenson has known Esther from her time in Hay-on-Wye.

Esther grew up in the Welsh borders. At Cambridge she edited *The Cambridge Review* and became a teaching fellow of Newnham College. She's mother to four remarkable sons (Edmund, writer and potter, is one). As 'Esther Moir' she wrote *The Discovery of Britain: The English Tourists 1540-1840*, and by the name Esther de Waal she's known for luminous writings on spirituality, and for *Living on the Border*. You'll notice that her poet-friends attend in their verse, as she does, to the people, the history and the physical actuality of the Marches, and that they discern wonderment within them.

These colloquies and friendships have given to today's poetry in Siluria a regional coherence and a characteristic voice.

This garland of poems

From mediaeval to modern, we've arranged poems by date. In date order too are the biographical notes on the lives of both poets and painters. The paintings sit more randomly, each on the page that best befits it.

The verses touch on the history or the loveliness of the Borderland. Some poems chuckle at our ways; some whisper gentle insights. A georgic tells how best to tend apple orchards; another how best to tend sheep. Particular poems express delight, even ecstasy; others are wry and shrewd. I expect you will find, as I do, that, garlanded together, they celebrate Siluria.

By Offa's Dyke Bryan Aspden recalled the turbulent history of the Marches. He searched, as we have, for *"words that would heal the hurt / of this land with its boundary at its heart".*

Jonathan Lumby

J.M.W. Turner,
*View of
Hampton Court
Herefordshire
from the
Southeast*
(Yale Center
for British Art)

WILLIAM OF WYCOMBE

Precentor of Leominster, 13th century

Sumer is icumen in –

Sumer is icumen in –
Lhude sing cuccu!   *loud*
Groweth sed and bloweth med   *seed; mead*
And springth the wude nu.   *wood*
Sing cuccu!

Awe bleteth after lomb,   *ewe; lamb*
Lhouth after calve cu,   *lows; cow*
Bulluc sterteth, bucke verteth.   *bullock; billy-goat; farts*
Murie sing cuccu,
Cuccu, cuccu!

Well singes thu, cuccu!
Ne swik thu naver nu!   *cease*

Sing cuccu nu! Sing cuccu!
Sing cuccu! Sing cuccu nu!
Sing cuccu nu! Sing cuccu!
Sing cuccu! Sing cuccu nu!

1

Sumer is icumen in
(British Library)

2

Brian Hatton,
*Miss Brenda
Wadworth*, 1911
(Hereford
Art Gallery

SIR JOHN CLANVOWE

of Hergest and Yazor, 1341-91

The Boke of Cupide, God of Love

Lovesickness is the theme of The Boke of Cupide. *The poet suffers grievously from love during sleepless nights in the month of May, so he rises early intent on hearing a nightingale, a bird of love. In a meadow beside a stream (perhaps in Yazor), he hears first the call of a cuckoo. Cuckoos are 'lewd' birds, tradition holds, because they lay eggs in other birds' nests. The poet listens entranced to a fraught discussion about love between a sweet-voiced nightingale and the two-toned cuckoo, the former romantic, the latter wry and down-to-earth. The cuckoo holds that it is wise to avoid the sickness, sorrow, envy, shame, jealousy and near madness that love inflicts. The poem teases – the cuckoo seems to win the argument. The poet of* The Boke of Cupide *delights in springtime and is tender towards those who love. In total the poem has 290 lines. This extract precedes the debate between the birds.*

3

For every trewe, gentil herte fre	*true, noble heart*	I speke this of felyng, trewely,	
That with him is, or thinketh for to be,		For al thogh I be olde and unlusty,	
Agens May now shal have somme steryng,	*toward; stirring*	Yet have I felt of that sekenes in May,	
Other to joy, or elles to morenynge,	*either; or else; mourning*	Bothe hote and colde, an accesse every day,	*an attack of fever*
In no seson so grette, as thynkes me.		How sore ywis ther wot no wight but I.	*no one knows better than me*
For when they mowe her the briddes sing,	*may hear; birds*	I am so shaken with the feveres white,	*wan love-sickness*
And see the floures and the leves spring,	*flowers; leaves*	Of al this May yet slept I but a lyte;	*little*
That bringes in to hertis remembraunce		And also hit is unlyke to me	
A maner ease, medled with grevaunce,	*ease mingled with regret*	That eny herte shulde slepy be,	*sleepy*
And lusty thoghtes ful of grete longynge,		In whom that love his firy dart wol smyte.	
And of that longynge cometh hevynesse,	*sorrow*	But as I lay this other nyght waking,	
And therof groues ofte grete seknesse,		I thoght how lovers had a tokenyng,	*saying*
And al for lak of that that they desyre;		And among hem hit was a comune tale,	*common*
And thus in May ben hertys set on fire,	*are hearts*	That hit wer good to her the nyghtyngale	*hear*
And so they brenne forthe in grete distresse.	*burn*	Rather than the leude cukkow syng.	*lewd (ill-mannered)*

And then I thoght anon as hit was day,
I wolde goo somme whedir for to assay   *somewhere else to try*
Yf that I myght a nyghtyngale here,
For yet I non had herd of al this yere;
And hit was tho the thirde nyght of May.

And anon as I the day espied,
No lenger wolde I in my bed abyde;   *I no longer wished*
But in to a wode that was fast by,   *wood*
I went forthe allone prively,   *forth alone secretly*
And helde my way don on a broke syde,   *down the bank of a brook*

Til I come in to a launde of white and grene,   *clearing*
So feire oon had I nevere inne bene.   *fair*
The grounde was grene, poudred with dayse,   *flecked with daisies*
The floures and the gras ilike hie,   *flowers; equally high*
Al grene and white was no thing elles sene.

4

Ther sat I doune amonge the feire floures
And sawe the briddes crepe out of her boures,   *bowers*
Ther as they had rested hem al nyght.
They were so joyful of the dayes lyght,
That they began of May to don her houres.   *do observances*
   (sing canonical hours)

They coude that servise alle bye rote.   *knew; by rote*
Ther was mony a lovely note:
Somme songe loude, as they had playned,   *had sung a basic melody*
And somme in other maner voys yfeyned,   *assumed (cf feigned)*
And somme al out, with al the fulle throte.

They pruned hem, and made hem ryght gay,   *preened themselves*
And daunseden, and lepten on the spray,   *danced; leapt*
And evermore two and two in fere,   *together*
Ryght so as they had chosen hem to yere   *just as; this year*
In March, uponn Seynt Valentynes day.

And the ryver that I sat upon,
Hit made such a noyse as hit ronne,
Acordaunt to the foules ermonye.   *harmony*
Me thoght hit was the beste melodye
That myghte ben yherd of eny man.

And for delyte therof, I note ner how,   *I don't know how*
I fel in such a slombre and a swowe –   *slumber; swoon*
Not al on slepe, ne fully wakynge –   *not completely asleep*
And in that swowe me thoght I herde singe
That sory bridde, the lewde cukkowe. . . .

5

Thomas Hearne,
*The River Teme
at Downton*,
1786
Illustration
from Richard
Payne Knight's
poem
The Landscapes

6

Christopher
Saxton,
*Hand-coloured
Map of
Herefordshire*,
1610
(British Library)

MICHAEL DRAYTON

Poly-Olbion (1622)
A Chorographical Description of all the Tracts, Rivers,
Mountains, Forests of this Renowned Isle of GREAT BRITAIN

Saint David's cell at Llanthony   4th Song 217-33

*Envoys from the West Country seek to enlist the support of the Welsh in the
struggle against Saxon advance. 'Hodney' is the River Honddu.*

. . The *Britons*, like devout, their messengers direct
To *David*, that he would their ancient right protect.
'Mongst *Hatterill's* lofty hills, that with the clouds are crown'd,
The Valley *Ewias* lies, immur'd so deep and round,
As they below that see the mountains rise so high,
Might think the straggling herds were grazing in the sky:
Which it in such a shape of solitude doth bear,
As Nature at the first appointed it for pray'r:
Where, in an aged Cell, with moss and ivy grown,
In which not to this day the sun hath ever shone,
That reverend *British* Saint, in zealous ages past,
To contemplation liv'd; and did so truly fast,
As he did only drink what crystal *Hodney* yields,
And fed upon the Leeks he gather'd in the fields.
In memory of whom, in the revolving year,
The Welch-men on his day that sacred herb do wear:
Where, of that holy man, as humbly they do crave,
That in their just defence they might his furtherance have.

7

John Sell Cotman,
Llanthony Abbey,
1801
(Tate Gallery)

8

C. Westwood,
*Hereford Wye
Bridge and
Cathedral*, 1890
(Hereford
Art Gallery)

The Excellency of Lemster Wool 7th Song 144ff

Drayton follows the course of the Lugg past Leominster.

Lug little *Oney* first, then *Arro* in doth take. . .
  Where lives the man so dull, on *Britain*'s further shore,
To whom did never sound the name of *Lemster* Ore?
That with the silkworm's web for smallness doth compare:
Wherein the winder shows his workmanship so rare . .
. . Of each in high'st accompt, and reckoned here as fine,
As there th'*Appulian* fleece, or dainty *Tarentyne*.
From thence his lovely self for *Wye* he doth dispose,
To view the goodly flocks on each hand as he goes.

Hereford and the Meeting of Lugg and Wye 7th Song 166-178
A great way he hath gone, and *Hereford* doth show
Her rising spires aloft; when as the princely *Wye*,
Him from his muse to wake, arrests him by and by.
Whose meeting to behold, with how well-ord'red grace
Each other entertains, how kindly they embrace;
For joy, so great a shout the bordering *City* sent
That with the sound thereof, which thorough *Haywood* went,
The Wood-Nymphs did awake that in the forest won;
To know the sudden cause, and presently they ron
With locks uncomb'd, for haste the lovely *Wye* to see
(The Flood that grac'd her most) this day should married be
To that more lovely *Lug*; a River of much fame,
That in her wandering banks should lose his glorious name.

9

Brian Hatton,
*Trees by bridge
over the Lugg,*
1905-6
(Hereford Art
Gallery)

The Marcle Landslip
7th Song 183-192

. . . But *Marcely*, grieved that he (the nearest of the rest,
And of the Mountain-kind) not bidden was a guest
Unto this nuptial feast, so hardly it doth take,
As (meaning for the same his station to forsake)
Inrag'd and mad with grief, himself in two did rive;
The trees and hedges near, before him up doth drive,
And dropping headlong down, three days together fall:
Which, bellowing as he went, the rocks did so appall,
That they him passage made, who cotes and chapels crush'd;
So violently he into his valley rush'd.

See page 32 for a note on the landslip of 1571, known as 'The Wonder'.

10

Poly-Olbion is one of the longest poems in the language – thirty songs, each of 400 lines. The songs are about the geography, legends and history of each county in the land. The poet, Michael Drayton, had access to Christopher Saxton's *Atlas of England and Wales* (1579). Saxton's county maps show rivers but no highways, and likewise Drayton patterns his poem around the courses of rivers, to each ascribing in fancy its own nymph or spirit. Drayton addresses a preface in *Poly-Olbion* to 'my friends the Cambro-Britons' (the Welsh). He explains that in the progress of the poem around English and Welsh counties he has striven to uphold the 'ancient bounds' of Wales, the 'Severne, and Dee'. Therefore, he states, 'I have included the parts of those three English Shires that lie on the West of Severne within their ancient mother Wales.'

Ross and the Golden Valley
7th Song 193-216

But *Wye* (from her dear *Lug* whom nothing can restrain,
In many a pleasant shade, her joy to entertain)
To *Rosse* her course directs; and right her name to show,
Oft windeth in her way, as back she meant to go.
Meander, who is said so intricate to be,
Hath not so many turns, nor crankling nooks as she.
    The *Herefordian* fields when well-near having pass'd
As she is going forth two sister Brooks at last
That soil her kindly sends, to guide her on her way;
Neat *Gamar*, that gets in swift *Garran*; which do lay
Their waters in one bank, augmenting of her train,
To grace the goodly *Wye*, as she doth pass by *Deane*.
    Beyond whose equal spring unto the West doth lie
The goodly *Golden Vale*, whose luscious scents do fly
More free than *Hybla's* sweets; and twixt her bordering hills,
The air with such delights and delicacy fills,
As makes it loth to stir, or thence those smells to bear.
Th'*Hesperides* scarce had such pleasure as be there: . . .
. . . Banks crown'd with curled Groves, from cold to keep the Plain,
Fields batful, flow'ry Meads, in state them to maintain.

11

Brian Hatton,
Lugg Meadows,
1906
(Hereford
Art Gallery)

'The Commonwealth' from Rowland Vaughan's book (Huntington Library, California)

12

JOHN DAVIES OF HEREFORD

from A Panegyricke

. . . But in His *Drownings*, He makes *Lands* arise,
In *grace* and *goodnesse* to the highest pitch;
And *Meades*, and *Pastures* price he multiplies;
So, while some lies, He rise doth in the *Ditch*.

His royall **TRENCH** (that all the rest commands
And holds the *Sperme* of *Herbage*) by a *Spring*
Infuseth in the wombe of sterile *Lands*,
The *Liquid seede* that makes them *Plenty* bring . . .

But o! this is not all thou dost behight
Deere *Vaughan*, thy Deere-Country for her good;
For, thou resolv'st to raise that benefit
Out of thy private care; and *Liv'lyhood*.

Thy many trades (too many to rehearse
That shall on thy *Foundation* stedfast stand)
Shall with their *Praiers*, still the *Heavens* pierce;
And blesse their *Founders* rare *Head*, *Heart*, and *Hand*!

That publike Table which thou wilt erect
(Where forty every Meale shall freely feed)
Will be the *Cause* of this so good *Effect*
To plant both *Trades* and *Trafficke* there with speed.

There shall thy Jovialist *Mechanicalls*
Attend this *Table* all in *Scarlet* Cappes;
(As if they were King *Arthures* Seneschals)
And, for their paines shall fill their *Chapps* and *Lapps*.

For, never since King *Arthurs* glorious dayes
(Whose radiant Knights did Ring his Table round)
Did any such a Table raise
As this, where *Viands* shall to all abound!

Nay *this*, shall that franke *Table* farre exceed
If we respect the good still done by each:
For, that fedde none but such as had no need;
But this (like God) shall feed both poore and rich!

Thy virtuous care to have thy God ador'd
(Among thy *Paines* and *Pleasures*) all will blesse:
Thy *Pension* for a Preacher of his Word,
Shewes thou seek'st Heaven, and earthly happinesse.

A *Chappell* and a *Curate* for the same
(The one maintain'd, the other built by Thee
For Gods Diurnall praise) shall make thy *Name*
In Rubricke of the *Saints* enrold to be.

Thine *Almes-house* for thy haplesse *Mechanicks*
Shall blaze thy charity to After-ages
And longer last in Brests of men, then Bricks;
Increasing still thy heavenly Masters Wages.

The *Drummes* and *Trumpets* (*Mars* his melodie)
That wonted were to call thy foes to fight,
Shall now but call a friendly Company
(For honest ends) to *feasting* and *delight*.

Glory of *Wales*, and luster of thy name,
That giv'st to both *sans* Parralel'd renowne,
Upon the *Poles* inscribed be thy *Fame*,
That it to *Worlds* unknown may still be knowne.

That they may say a Nooke but of an *Isle*
That Northward lies, doth yield a rarer Man,
Then larger Lands by many a Thousand Mile,
Who can do Thus, and will do what He can.

behight promise; *hight* named; *chapps* jaws, chops;
franke generous; *hen* than;
who can do thus who can do just as he has described

Rowland Vaughan, born in Bredwardine, had an estate along the River Dore. John Davies extols Vaughan's plan to dig irrigation channels and mill-leats in the Golden Valley, and to establish a utopian commune. Vaughan held that 'The Golden Vale' was 'the Lombardy of Herefordshire, the Garden of old Gallants, and the Paradise of the whole Principality'. He proposed 'to raise a golden world in the Golden-Vale of Herefordshire bordering on Wales . . .being the richest, yet (for want of imployment) the plentifullest place of poore in the Kingdome.'

In his book *Most Approved, and Long experienced Water Workes, etc* (1610), Vaughan explains that the community of 200 would be self-sufficient; mills would supply power to workshops of dozens of craftsmen; good food and cheer would be provided at shared tables, diners being summoned by trumpets; a chapel would be built, a priest installed. Vaughan believed his meadow would be 'ten-fold' more profitable when irrigated.

In the Golden Valley today you can see the pattern of Vaughan's 'drownings' – his 'Royal Trench', 'Counter Trenches', ' Winter and Summer Trenches', and so on. Litigation sapped Vaughan's funds; probably he never built the dwellings and workshops. Yet his proposals prefigure the communitarian ideals of Gerrard Winstanley and the Diggers in the late 1640s and the utopian schemes of Robert Owen in New Lanark and New Harmony in the early 1800s.

HENRY VAUGHAN the Silurist

The Retreate

Happy those early dayes! when I
Shin'd in my Angell-infancy.
Before I understood this place
Appointed for my second race,
Or taught my soul to fancy ought
But a white, Celestiall thought,
When yet I had not walkt above
A mile, or two, from my first love,
And looking back (at that short space,)
Could see a glimpse of his bright face;
When on some *gilded Cloud*, or *flowre*
My gazing soul would dwell an houre,
And in those weaker glories spy
Some shadows of eternity;
Before I taught my tongue to wound
My Conscience with a sinfull sound,
Or had the black art to dispence

A sev'rall sinne to ev'ry sence,
But felt through all this earthly dresse
Bright *shootes* of everlastingnesse.

O how I long to travell back
And tread again that ancient track!
That I might once more reach that plaine,
Where first I left my glorious traine,
From whence th'Inlightned spirit sees
That shady City of Palme trees;
But (ah!) my soul with too much stay
Is drunk, and staggers in the way.
Some men a forward motion love,
But I by backward steps would move,
And when this dust falls to the urn
In that state I came return.

from *Silex Scintillans* 1650

14

15

Joseph Murray
Ince,
*Hay-on-Wye
and the
Brecon Beacons*,
1846
(Llyfrgell
Genedlaethol
Cymru/
National Library
of Wales)

The Morning-watch

O Joyes! Infinite sweetnes! with what flowres,
And shoots of glory, my soul breakes, and buds!
    All the long houres
    Of night, and Rest
    Through the still shrouds
    Of sleep, and Clouds,
    This Dew fell on my Breast;
    O how it *Blouds*,
And *Spirits* all my Earth! heark! In what Rings,
And *Hymning Circulations* the quick world
    Awakes, and sings;
    The rising winds,
    And falling springs,
    Birds, beasts, all things
    Adore him in their kinds.
    Thus all is hurl'd
In sacred *Hymnes*, and *Order*, The great *Chime*
And *Symphony* of nature. Prayer is
    The world in tune,
    A spirit-voyce
    And vocall joys
    Whose *Eccho* is heav'ns blisse.
    O let me climbe
When I lye down! The Pious soul by night
Is like a clouded starre, whose beames though sed
    To shed their light
    Under some Cloud
    Yet are above,
    And shine, and move
    Beyond that mistie shrowd.

    So in my Bed
That Curtain'd grave, though sleep, like ashes, hide
My lamp, and life, both shall in thee abide.

from *Silex Scintillans* 1650

Blouds   bloods, invigorates

The World (1650)

I saw Eternity the other night
Like a great Ring of pure and endless light,
   All calm, as it was bright,
And round beneath it, Time in hours, days, years
   Driv'n by the spheres
Like a vast shadow mov'd, in which the world
   And all her train were hurl'd . . . .

17

Joshua Cristall,
*A Cottage
on the side of
Symonds Yat,
near Goodrich,*
1825
(Museum and
Art Gallery,
Bolton)

18

John Sell
Cotman,
*Crickhowell,
Breconshire*,
c.1800
(Yale Center
for British Art)

To the River Isca

Henry
Vaughan

. . . But *Isca*, whenso'er those shades I see,
And thy lov'd Arbours must no more know me,
When I am layd to rest hard by thy streams,
And my Sun sets, where first it sprang in beams,
I'le leave behind me such a large, kind, light,
As shall redeem thee from oblivious night,
And in these vowes which (living yet) I pay
Shed such a Previous and Enduring Ray,
As shall from age to age thy fair name lead
'Till Rivers leave to run, and men to read.
First, may all Bards born after me
(When I am ashes) sing of thee!
May thy green banks and streams (or none)
Be both their Hill and Helicon;
May Vocall Groves grow there, and all
The shades in them Propheticall,
Where (laid) men shall more faire truths see
Than fictions were of Thessalie;
May thy gentle Swains (like flowres)
Sweetly spend their Youthfull houres
And thy beauteous Nymphs (like Doves)
Be kind and faithfull to their Loves;
Garlands, and Songs, and Roundelayes,
Mild, dewie nights, and Sun-shine dayes,
The Turtles voice, Joy without fear,
Dwell on thy bosome all the year!

May the Evet and the Tode
Within thy Banks have no abode,
Nor the wilie, winding Snake
Her voyage through the waters make.
In all thy Journey to the Main
No nitrous Clay, nor Brimstone-vein
Mixe with thy streams, but may they passe
Fresh as the aire, and cleer as Glasse,
And where the wandring Chrystal treads
Roses shall kisse, and Couple heads.
The factour-wind from far shall bring
The Odours of the Scatter'd Spring,
   And loaden with the rich Arreare,
Spend it in Spicie whispers there.
No sullen heats, nor flames that are
Offensive, and Canicular,
Shine on thy Sands, nor pry to see
Thy Scalie, shading familie,
But Noones as mild as Hesper's rayes,
Or the first blushes of fair dayes.
What gifts more Heav'n or Earth can adde
With all those blessings be thou Clad! . . . .

from *Olor Iscanus* 1647

19

Isca   the River Usk
evet   newt
factour   merchant
canicular of the hot season of the dog-star

20

John Varley,
*Brecon on the
River Usk*, 1837
(Brecknock
Museum
and Art Gallery)

Ad fluvium Iscam

Isca, parens florum, placido qui spumeus ore
    Lambis lapillos aureos,
Qui mœstos hyacinthos, & picti ἄνθεα tophi
    Mulces susurris humidis,
Dumque novas pergunt menses Consumere Lunas
    Cœlumque mortales terit,
Accumulas cum Sole dies, œvumque per omne
    Fidelis Induras latex,
O quis Inaccessos & quali murmure lucos
    Mutumque; Solaris nemus!
Per te discerpti credo Thracis ire querelas
    Plectrumque divini senis.

from *Olor Iscanus* 1647

Kind Usk, among thy flowers, whose wave
Golden pebbles still doth lave;
With dewy whisper making glad
The primrose and the bluebell sad;
While moons lead time his destined way
And men expire, yet day by day
In the sun the same as ever,
An unconquerable River,
So divine's thy murmuring hymn
To these woodlands tall and dim
That I think I hear on thee
Orpheus' deep-drawn melody,
His sweet strings resounding clear,
His ancient magic echoing here.

Translation by Edmund Blunden

Retirement

Fresh fields and woods! The Earth's fair face,
God's foot-stool, and man's dwelling-place.
I ask not why the first Believer
Did love to be a Country liver,
Who to secure pious content
Did pitch by groves and wells his tent;
Where he might view the boundless skie,
And all those glorious lights on high:
With flying meteors, mists and show'rs,
Subjected hills, trees, meads and Flow'rs:
And ev'ry minute bless the King
And wise Creatour of each thing.
  I ask not why he did remove
To happy Mamre's holy grove,
Leaving the Cities of the plain
To Lot and his successless train.
All various Lusts in Cities still
Are found; they are the Thrones of Ill.
The dismal Sinks, where blood is spill'd,
Cages with much uncleanness fill'd.
But rural shades are the sweet fense
Of piety and innocence.
They are the Meek's kind region, where
Angels descend, and rule the sphere:
Where heaven lies Leiguer, and the Dove
Duely as Dew, comes from above.
If Eden be on Earth at all,
'Tis that, which we the Country call.

from *Thalia Rediviva* 1678

21

THOMAS TRAHERNE

from Centuries of Meditation
section 3.3

Traherne recalls how the world appeared to him when he was a young child. The street *and the* gates *must be those of Hereford and the* temple *Hereford Cathedral. Traherne puts this prose-poem into verse in the poem* Wonder.

The corn was orient and immortal wheat, which never should be reaped, nor was ever sown. I thought it had stood from everlasting to everlasting. The dust and stones of the street were as precious as gold. The gates were at first the end of the world. The green trees when I saw them first through one of the gates transported and ravished me; their sweetness and unusual beauty made my heart to leap, and almost mad with ecstasy, they were such strange and wonderful things. The Men! O what venerable and reverend creatures did the aged seem! Immortal Cherubims! And young men glittering and sparkling angels, and maids strange seraphic pieces of life and beauty! Boys and girls tumbling in the street, and playing, were moving jewels: I knew not that they were born or should die. But all things abided eternally as they were in their proper places. Eternity was manifest in the Light of the Day, and something infinite behind everything appeared, which talked with my expectation and moved my desire. The City seemed to stand in Eden, or to be built in Heaven. The streets were mine, the temple was mine, the people were mine, their clothes and gold and silver was mine, as much as their sparkling eyes, fair skins and ruddy faces. The skies were mine, and so were the sun and moon and stars, and all the world was mine; and I the only spectator and enjoyer of it. I knew no churlish proprieties, nor bounds nor divisions; but all proprieties and divisions were mine, all treasures and the possessors of them. So that with much ado I was corrupted, and made to learn the dirty devices of this world, which I now unlearn, and become, as it were, a little child again that I may enter into the Kingdom of God.

orient rising
proprieties owned land, property
so that with much ado but later with much effort

23

William Ward
Gill,
*Hereford
from Venns Lane*,
1852
(Hereford
Art Gallery)

Wonder

How like an angel came I down!
　　How bright are all things here!
When first among His works I did appear
　　O how their Glory me did crown!
The world resembled his *Eternity*,
　　In which my soul did walk;
And every thing that I did see,
　　Did with me talk.

The skies in their magnificence,
　　The lively, lovely air,
Oh how divine, how soft, how sweet, how fair!
　　The stars did entertain my sense,
And all the works of God, so bright and pure,
　　So rich and great did seem,
As if they ever must endure,
　　In my esteem.

A native health and innocence
　　Within my bones did grow,
And while my God did all his Glories show,
　　I felt a vigour in my sense
That was all Spirit. I within did flow
　　With seas of life, like wine;
I nothing in the world did know,
　　But 'twas divine.

Harsh ragged objects were concealed,
　　Oppressions, tears, and cries,
Sins, griefs, complaints, dissensions, weeping eyes
　　Were hid, and only things revealed
Which heavenly Spirits, and the Angels prize.
　　The state of Innocence
And bliss, not trades and poverties,
　　Did fill my sense.

The streets were paved with golden stones,
　　The boys and girls were mine,
Oh how did all their lovely faces shine!
　　The sons of men were holy ones,
In joy and beauty they appeared to me,
　　And every thing which here I found,
While like an angel I did see,
　　Adorned the ground.

Rich diamond and pearl and gold
　　In every place was seen;
Rare splendours, yellow, blue, red, white and green,
　　Mine eyes did everywhere behold.
Great wonders clothed with glory did appear,
　　Amazement was my bliss,
That and my wealth was everywhere;
　　No joy to this!

Cursed and devised proprieties,
　　With envy, avarice
And fraud, those fiends that spoil even Paradise,
　　Flew from the splendour of mine eyes.
And so did hedges, ditches, limits, bounds,
　　I dreamed not aught of those,
　　But wandered over all men's grounds,
　　　And found repose.
　Proprieties themselves were mine,
　　And hedges ornaments;

Walls, boxes, coffers, and their rich contents
　　Did not divide my joys, but all combine.
Clothes, ribbons, jewels, laces, I esteemed
　　My joys by others worn:
　　For me they all to wear them seemed
　　　When I was born.

The Salutation

These little limbs,
These eyes and hands which here I find,
These rosy cheeks wherewith my life begins,
Where have ye been? behind
What curtains were ye from me hid so long!
Where was, in what abyss, my speaking tongue ?

When silent I,
So many thousand, thousand years,
Beneath the dust did in a chaos lie,
How could I smiles or tears,
Or lips or hands or eyes or ears perceive?
Welcome, ye treasures which I now receive.

I that so long
Was nothing from eternity,
Did little think such joys as ear or tongue,
To celebrate or see:
Such sounds to hear, such hands to feel, such feet,
Beneath the skies on such a ground to meet.

New burnisht joys!
Which yellow gold and pearl excel!
Such sacred treasures are the limbs in boys,
In which a soul doth dwell;
Their organised joints and azure veins
More wealth include than all the world contains.

From dust I rise,
And out of nothing now awake,
These brighter regions which salute mine eyes,
A gift from God I take.
The earth, the seas, the light, the day, the skies,
The sun and stars are mine; if those I prize.

Long time before
I in my mother's womb was born,
A God preparing did this glorious store,
The world, for me adorn.
Into this Eden so divine and fair,
So wide and bright, I come His son and heir.

A stranger here
Strange things doth meet, strange glories see;
Strange treasures lodg'd in this fair world appear;
Strange all, and new to me.
But that they mine should be, who nothing was,
That strangest is of all, yet brought to pass.

27

David Cox,
Lugg Meadows,
near Hereford,
date uncertain
(Victoria
and Albert
Museum)

John Philips

from Cyder (1708)

*Cyder is a long poem which instructs on the cultivation of apples and the making of cider.
It celebrates the orchards of Herefordshire and those who tend them.*

Nature's Gifts   Bk 1: 1-10

What Soil the Apple loves, what Care is due
To Orchats, timeliest when to press the Fruits,
Thy Gift, *Pomona*, in *Miltonian* Verse
Adventrous I presume to sing; of Verse
Nor skill'd, nor studious: But my Native Soil
Invites me, and the Theme as yet unsung.

  Ye *Ariconian* Knights, and fairest Dames
To whom propitious Heav'n these Blessings grants,
Attend my Layes; nor hence distain to learn,
How Nature's Gifts may be improv'd by Art . . .

Pomona   goddess of fruit and orchards
Ariconian   of Herefordshire. Ariconium, a 'lost' Roman city,
    was once thought to have been at Kenchester but is now
    located east of Penyard.

28

How to Choose Land for an Orchard   1: 20-40

. . . Who-e'er expects his lab'ring Trees shou'd bend
With Fruitage, and a kindly Harvest yield,
Be this his first Concern; to find a Tract
Impervious to the Winds, begirt with Hills,
That intercept the *Hyperborean* Blasts
Tempestuous, and cold *Eurus* nipping Force,
Noxious to feeble Buds; But to the West
Let him free Entrance grant, let *Zephyrs* bland
Administer their tepid genial Airs;
Naught fear he from the West, whose gentle Warmth
Discloses well Earth's all-teeming Womb,
Invigorating tender Seeds; Whose Breath
Nurtures the *Orange*, and the *Citron* Groves,
Hesperian Fruits, and wafts their Odours sweet
Wide thro' the Air, and distant Shores perfumes.
Nor only do the Hills exclude the Winds:
But, when the blackning Clouds in sprinkling Show'rs
Distill, from the high Summits down the Rain
Runs trickling; with the fertile Moisture chear'd
The Orchats smile: joyous the Farmers see
Their thriving Plants, and bless the heav'nly Dew.

Hyperborean   extreme northerly
Hesperian   Spanish, or of the fabled Garden of the Hesperides

29

Gilbert Spencer,
*Orchard
at Tarrington,*
1961
(Hereford
Art Gallery)

Adapting to the soil   1:41-77

Next, let the Planter, with Discretion meet,
The Force and Genius of each Soil explore;
To what adapted, what it shuns averse:
Without this necessary Care, in vain
He hopes an Apple-Vintage, and invokes
Pomona's Aid in vain. The miry Fields,
Rejoycing in rich Mold, most ample Fruit
Of beauteous Form produce; pleasing to Sight,
But to the Tongue inelegant and flat.
So Nature has decreed; so, oft we see
Men passing fair, in outward Lineaments
Elaborate; less, inwardly, exact.
Nor from the sable Ground expect Success,
Nor from cretaceous, stubborn and jejune:
The Must, of pallid Hue, declares the Soil
Devoid of Spirit; wretched He, that quaffs
Such wheyish Liquors; oft with Colic Pangs,
With pungent Colic Pangs distress'd, he'll roar
And toss, and turn, and curse th'unwholsome Draught.
But, Farmer, look, where full-eared Sheaves of Rye
Grow wavy on the Tilth, that soil select
For Apples; thence thy Industry shall gain,
Ten-fold Reward; thy Garners, thence with Store
Surcharg'd, shall burst; thy Press with purest Juice
Shall flow, which, in revolving Years, may try
Thy feeble Feet, and bind thy fault'ring Tongue.
Such is *Kentchurch*, such *Dantzeyan* Ground,
Such thine, O learned *Brome*, and *Capel* such,
Willisian Burlton, much loved *Geers* his *Marsh*,
And *Sutton*-Acres, drenched with Regal Blood
Of *Ethelbert*, when to th'unhallow'd Feast
Of *Mercian Offa* he invited came,

To treat of Spousals: Long connubial Joys
He promis'd to himself, allured by Fair
Elfrida's Beauty; but deluded dy'd
In height of Hopes – Oh! Hardest Fate, to fall
By Shew of Friendship, and pretended Love!

sable ground black earth
cretaceous chalky
must juice prepared for fermentation
Kentchurch In Ewyas Harold, the home of the Scudamore
    family *Dantzeyan Ground* Brinsop, the home of William
    Dansey (1665-1708)
Brome William Brome (1664-1745), antiquary of Ewithington
Capel King's Capel and How Capel, presumed by Philips to be
    ancestral lands of Algernon Capel, 2nd Earl of Essex
Willisian Burlton Burlton Court in Burghill, home of the
    scholar Browne Willis (1682-1760)
Geers Timothy Geers of The Marsh, near Bridge Sollers
Sutton Acres The supposed site of Offa's palace in Sutton St
    Michael. In 794 Ethelbert, King of the East Angles, came
    as Offa's guest hoping to marry Elfrida. Here he was slain.

31

John Varley,
*View of
Bodenham
and the
Malvern Hills,*
1801
(Tate Gallery)

The Wandering Glebe of Marcley Hill   1:78-88

I nor advise, nor reprehend the Choice
Of *Marcley*-Hill; the Apple no where finds
A kinder Mold: Yet 'tis unsafe to trust
Deceitful Ground: Who knows but that, once more,
This Mount may journey, and, his present site
Forsaking, to thy Neighbours Bounds transfer
The goodly Plants, affording Matter strange
For Law-Debates? If, therefore, thou incline
To deck this Rise with Fruits of various Tastes
Fail not by frequent Vows t'implore Success;
Thus piteous Heav'n may fix the wand'ring Glebe.

William Camden in *Britannia* (tr. Philemon Holland, 1610)
wrote of the landslip which buried Kinnaston Church and cot-
tages nearby: '*Neere unto the place where Lug and Wy meet together,
Eastward, a hill which they call Marcley Hill, in the yere of our
redemption 1571 (as though it had wakened upon the sodaine out
of a deepe sleepe) roused itself up, and for the space of three daies
together moving and shewing it selfe (as mighty and huge a heape
as it was) with roring noise in a fearfull sort, and overturning all
things that stood in the way, advanced itself forward to the wonderous
astonishment of the beholders.'* The site of the landslip is still known
as 'The Wonder'. Christopher Saxton on his map (1577) marks
the place: '*Kinnaston chap: Wch was dreven downe by the removing
of the ground*'.

How to Graft   1:273-311

  Wouldst thou, thy Vats with gen'rous Juice should froth?
Respect thy Orchats; think not, that the Trees
Spontaneous will produce an wholesome Draught.
Let Art correct thy Breed: from Parent Bough
A Cyon meetly sever; after, force
A way into the Crabstock's close-wrought Grain
By Wedges, and within the living Wound
Enclose the Foster Twig; nor over-nice
Refuse with thy own Hands around to spread
The binding Clay: Ee'r-long their differing Veins
Unite, and kindly Nourishment convey
To the new Pupil; now he shoots his Arms
With quickest Growth; now shake the teeming Trunc,
Down rain th'impurpl'd Balls, ambrosial Fruit.
Whether the Wilding's Fibres are contriv'd
To draw th'Earth's purest Spirit, and resist
Its Feculence, which in more porous Stocks
Of Cyder-Plants finds Passage free, or else
The native Verjuice of the Crab, deriv'd
Thro' th'infix'd Graff, a grateful Mixture forms
Of tart and sweet; whatever be the Cause,
This doubtful Progeny by nicest Tastes
Expected best Acceptance finds, and pays
Largest Revenues to the Orchat-Lord.

  Some think, the *Quince* and *Apple* wou'd combine
In happy Union; Others fitter deem
The *Sloe*-Stem bearing Sylvan Plums austere.
Who knows but Both may thrive? Howe'er, what loss
To try the Pow'rs of Both, and search how far
Two different Natures may concur to mix
 In close Embraces, and strange Off-spring bear?

Thou't find that Plants will frequent Changes try,
Undamag'd, and their marriageable Arms
Conjoin with others. So *Silurian* Plants
Admit the *Peache*'s odiferous Globe,
And *Pears* of sundry Forms; at diff'rent times
Adopted *Plums* will aliene Branches grace;
And Men have gather'd from the *Hawthorn's* Branch
Large *Medlars*, imitating regal Crowns.

cyon scion
crabstock crab-apple
wilding crab-apple
Silurian from Herefordshire. Philips again uses the word
   Silurian in the last words of the long poem:

   '. . . to the utmost Bounds of this
   Wide Universe, *Silurian* Cyder borne
   Shall please all tastes, and triumph o'er the Vine.'

33

Joshua Cristall,
*A Herefordshire
Lady*, 1839
(Hereford
Art Gallery)

Varieties of Apple   1: 457-478

  Now turn thine Eye to view *Alcinous'* Groves,
The Pride of the *Phoeacian* Isle, from whence,
Sailing the Spaces of the boundless Deep,
To *Ariconium* pretious Fruits arriv'd:
The *Pippin* burnish'd o'er with Gold, the *Moile*
Of sweetest hony'd Taste, the fair *Permain*,
Temper'd, like comliest Nymph, with red and white.
Salopian Acres florish with a Growth
Peculiar, styl'd the *Ottley*: Be thou first
This Apple to transplant; if to the Name
It's Merit answers, no where shalt thou find
A Wine more priz'd, or laudable of Taste.
Nor does the *Eliot* least deserve thy Care,
Nor *John-Apple*, whose wither'd Rind, entrencht
With many a Furrow, aptly represents
Decrepid Age; nor that from *Harvey* nam'd,
Quick-relishing: Why should we sing the *Thrift,*
Codling, or *Pomroy*, or of pimpled Coat
The *Russet*, or the *Cats-Head's* weighty Orb,
Enormous in its Growth; for various Use
Tho' these are meet, tho' after full repast
Are oft requir'd, and crown the rich Desert?

Pear Trees   1:479-494

  What, tho' the *Pear*-Tree rival not the Worth
Of *Ariconian* Products? Yet her Freight
Is not contemn'd, yet her wide-branching Arms
Best screen thy Mansion from the fervent Dog
Averse to Life; the wintry Hurricanes
In vain imploy their Roar, her Trunc unmov'd
Breaks the strong Onset, and controls their Rage.
Chiefly the *Bosbury*, whose large Increase,
Annual, in sumptuous Banquets claims Applause.
Thrice acceptable Bev'rage! could but Art
Subdue the floating Lee, *Pomona's* self
Would dread thy Praise, and shun the dubious Strife.
Be it thy Choice, when Summer-Heats annoy,
To sit beneath her leafy Canopy,
Quaffing rich Liquids: Oh! How sweet t'enjoy
At once her Fruits, and hospitable Shade!

Herefordshire Pomona,
Pomeroy

1. Pomeroy

The Musk and the Red-Streak

But how with equal Numbers shall we match
The *Musk*'s surpassing Worth! that earliest gives
Sure hopes of racy Wine, and in its Youth,
Its tender Nonage, loads the spreading Boughs
With large and juicy Off-spring, that defies
The Vernal Nippings, and cold Syderal Blasts!
Yet let her to the *Read-streak* yield, that once
Was of the Sylvan Kind, unciviliz'd,
Of no Regard, 'till *Scudamore*'s skilful Hand
Improv'd her, and by courtly Discipline
Taught her the savage Nature to forget:
Hence styl'd the *Scudamorean* Plant; whose Wine
Who-ever tastes, let him with grateful Heart
Respect that ancient loyal House, and wish
The noble Peer, that now transcends our Hopes
In early Worth, his Country's justest Pride,
Uninterrupted Joy, and Health entire.
Let every Tree in every Garden own

The *Red-streak* as supream; whose pulpous Fruit
With Gold irradiate, and Vermilian shines
Tempting, not fatal, as the Birth of that
Primaeval interdicted Plant, that won
Fond *Eve* in hapless Hour to taste, and die.
This, of more bounteous Influence, inspires
Poetic Raptures, and the lowly Muse
Kindles to loftier Strains; even I perceive
Her sacred Virtue. See! The Numbers flow
Easie, whilst, chear'd with her nectareous Juice
Hers, and my Country's Praises I exalt.
Hail *Herefordian* Plant, that dost distain
All other Fields! Heav'n's sweetest Blessing, hail!
Be thou the copious Matter of my Song,
And Thy choice *Nectar*; on which always waits
Laughter, and Sport, and care-beguiling Wit,
And Friendship, chief Delight of Human Life.
What shou'd we wish for more? Or why, in quest
Of foreign vintage, insincere and mixt,
Traverse th'extremest world?

Alcinous King of the Phaeacians. His orchard is described in the *Odyssey*
The Dog Sirius, the dog-star
The Musk a pear called the musk-apple
Scudamorean plant the Redstreak, much-praised cider-apple, grown at
    Holme Lacy by John Scudamore, 1st Viscount Scudamore (1601-
    71), who propagated it from a pip he brought home from France
    while Ambassador there. After Scudamore's time, the Redstreak
    declined in quality. *Pomona Herefordiensis* (1811) would record: 'trees
    of the Red-streak can now no longer be propagated; and the fruit,
    like the trees, is affected by the debilitated old age of the variety.'

Herefordshire Pomona,
Redstreak

Joshua Cristall, *The Gleaners,*
Betsy Southern, Coppet Hill,
1826 (Haworth Gallery, Accrington)

Joys of the Cider Harvest  2:363-395

John
Phili

The Farmer's Toil is done; his Cades mature,
Now call for Vent, his Lands exhaust permit
T'indulge awhile. Now solemn Rites he pays
To *Bacchus*, Author of Heart-cheering Mirth.
His honest Friends, at thirsty hour of Dusk,
Come uninvited; he with bounteous Hand
Imparts his smoking Vintage, sweet Reward
Of his own Industry; the well fraught Bowl
Circles incessant, whilst the humble Cell

With quavering Laugh, and rural Jest resounds.
Ease, and Content, and undissembled Love
Shine in each Face; the Thoughts of Labour past
Encrease their Joy. As, from retentive cage
When sullen *Philomel* escapes, her Notes
She varies, and of past Imprisonment
Sweetly complains; her Liberty retriev'd
Cheers her sad soul, improves her pleasing Song,
Gladsome they quaff, yet not exceed the Bounds
Of healthy Temp'rance, nor incroach on Night,
Season of Rest, but well bedew'd repair
Each to his Home, with unsupplanted Feet.
E'er Heav'n's emblazon'd by the rosie Dawn,
Domestic Cares awake them; brisk they rise,
Refresh'd, and lively with the Joys that flow
From amicable Talk, and moderate Cups
Sweetly interchang'd.

Cades casks
vent broaching
Philomel a nightingale

Summer's carousals and winter's jollities   2:400-434

. . . Thus to the generous Bottle all incline,
By parching Thirst allur'd: With vehement Suns
When dusty Summer bakes the crumbling Clods,
How pleasant is't, beneath the twisted Arch
Of a retreating Bow'r, in Mid-day's Reign
To ply the sweet Carouse, remote from Noise,
Secur'd of fev'rish Heats! When th'aged Year
Inclines, and Boreas' Spirit blusters frore,
Beware th'inclement Heav'ns; now let thy Hearth
Crackle with juiceless Boughs; thy lingering Blood
Now instigate with th'Apples powerful Streams.
Perpetual Showers, and stormy Gusts confine
The willing Ploughman, and December warms
To Annual Jollities; now sportive Youth
Carol incondite Rhythms, with suiting Notes,
And quaver unharmonious; sturdy Swains
In clean Array, for rustic Dance prepare,
Mixt with the Buxom Damsels; hand in hand
They frisk, and bound, and various Mazes weave,
Shaking their brawny Limbs, with uncouth Mein,
Transported, and sometimes, an oblique Leer
Dart on their Loves, sometimes a hasty Kiss
Steal from unwary Lasses; they with Scorn
And Neck reclin'd, resent the ravish'd Bliss.
Mean while, blind *British* Bards with volant Touch
Traverse loquacious Strings, whose solemn Notes
Provoke to harmless Revels; these among,

Joshua Cristall, *Fern Burners Reposing,*
Coppett Hill, 1828
(Dyer Collection)

John Philips

A subtle Artist stands, with wondrous Bag
That bears imprison'd Winds, (of gentler sort
Than those, which erst *Laertes* Son enclos'd.)
Peaceful they sleep, but let the tuneful Squeeze
Of labouring Elbow rouse them, out they fly
Melodious, and with spritely Accents charm.
'Midst these Disports, forget they not to drench
Themselves with bellying Goblets.. . .

Boreas' spirit the north wind
frore intensely cold
Laertes' son Homer in the *Odyssey* tells that Odysseus was the son of
Laertes, king of Ithaca. Odysseus was once entertained by Aeolus,
appointed by Zeus custodian of the winds. Aeolus gave Odysseus
a bag containing winds which might fill his sails. Philips compares
Odysseus' bag to a bagpipe played in Herefordshire at a revel.

38

Herefordshire Pomona,
The Yellow Eliot

James Cecil   1:608-620

Thee also, Glorious Branch of *Cecil*'s Line
This Country claims; with Pride and Joy to Thee
Thy *Alterennis* calls: yet she endures
Patient Thy Absence, since Thy prudent Choice
Has fix'd Thee in the Muse's fairest Seat,
Where *Aldrich* reigns, and from his endless Store
Of universal Knowledge still supplies
His noble Care; he generous Thoughts instills
Of true Nobility, their Country's Love,
(Chief End of Life) and forms their ductile Minds
To Human Virtues; By His Genius led,
Thou soon in every Art preeminent
Shalt grace this Isle, and rise to *Burleigh*'s Fame.

Cecil James Cecil, 5th Earl of Salisbury, a student at Christ
Church, Oxford, Philip's college
Alterennis Allt-yr-ynys, a manor-house at the confluence of
the Honddu and Monnow. The family of Cecil (formerly
'Sitsylt') originated from that house. William Cecil, Lord
Burghley (or Burleigh), chief adviser to Queen Elizabeth,
was James Cecil's great forebear.
Aldrich Henry Aldrich, Dean of Christ Church, Oxford
from 1689 to 1710

Robert Harley 1:652-666

But who is He, that on the winding Stream
Of *Vaga* first drew vital Breath, and now
Approv'd in *Anna's* secret Councils sits,
Weighing the Sum of Things, with wise Forecast
Sollicitous of public Good? How large
His Mind, that comprehends what-e'er was known
To Old, or Present Time; yet not elate,
Not conscious of its Skill? What Praise deserves
His liberal Hand, that gathers but to give,
Preventing Suit? O not unthankful Muse,
Him lowly reverence, that first deigned to hear
Thy Pipe, and skreen'd thee from opprobrious Tongues.
Acknowledge thy Own *Harley*, and his Name
Inscribe on ev'ry Bark; the wounded Plants
Will fast increase, faster thy just Respect.

Vaga the river Wye
Anna Queen Anne

Robert Harley (1661-1724) of Eywood and Brampton Bryan
was First Minister in Queen Anne's reign and most eminent
statesmen. In 1711 he became the Earl of Oxford and Lord
Mortimer. Harley enjoyed the company of writers. From 1704
he collected historical manuscripts. His first purchase was 600
that had belonged to Sir Simonds D'Ewes. He and his son eagerly
augmented this with mediaeval European and English documents. In 1753 the Harley family made their library available to
the British Museum at its founding. The Harleian Collection in
today's British Library comprises 7,000 manuscripts, 14,000 char-
ters and 500 rolls. *Sumer is icomen in* is listed as *Harley 978 f. 11v*

39

Sir Godfrey
Kneller,
*Robert Harley,
First Earl
of Oxford,*
c.1711
(Hereford
Art Gallery)

WILLIAM DIAPER

from Dryades (1712)

A pastoral scene reveals Pomona and nymphs mourning the death of Thyrsis – who is John Philips.

My heedless Steps had touch'd the hallow'd Ground,
Where airy Daemons dance the wanton Round;
Where fairy Elves, and mid-night Dryads meet,
And to the smiling Moon the Sylvan-Song repeat.
Tall rifted Oaks, and circling Elms had made
A Central void amidst surrounding Shade,
With hollow vaulted Cells, and rising Heaps
In which by Day the weary'd Badger sleeps.
Thick thorny Brakes grew round the lonesome Place,
And twining Boughs enclos'd the middle Space.
Here Dryads in nocturnal Revels join,
While Stars thro' shaking Leaves obscurely shine.
And here I saw (blessed with a kinder Fate)
When in a beauteous Ring the Nymphs were sate.
Well-pleased the Elphins smil'd, but she who guards
Pomaceous Fruits, and th'Orchet-Care rewards,

Down pensive lean'd her Head; no ruddy streaks
Mixt with the languid Paleness of her Cheeks.
Cast on the Ground her wither'd Garland lay,
Whose shrivell'd Leaves seem'd conscious of Decay.
Thyrsis, that much-love'd Youth, the Goddess mourn'd,
Thyrsis, who once Silurian Plains adorn'd;
The rural Pow'rs confess'd their meaner Lays,
When Thyrsis sung, and own'd his juster Praise;
He Ariconian Swains industrious taught
To strain rich Must, and press the racy Draught;
Since he is gone, the Trees are all decay'd,
With Moss bedight, and Blossoms ill-array'd
The pensive Owner mourns the tedious Weeks,
And wants the gen'rous Bowl, that paints the flushing Cheeks.

She who guards pomaceous fruits the goddess Pomona
Thyrsis a classical name for a pastoral singer. Thyrsis here represents
    John Philips, author of *Cyder*, who had died in 1709 aged 33.

41

Joshua Cristall,
Arcadian Landscape,
1830
(Tate Gallery)

William Boyce

The Herefordshire Winter (1730)

William Boyce composed the song's music.
We do not know who wrote the words.

At *Ross* how alter'd is the Scene!
  Lo, *Penyard*'s Beauties fail!
Lost is his Crown of smiling Green,
  And Fogs his Summit veil:
Old Wye, his mazy Course restrain'd,
  Lies o'er his Urn supine;
In Ice his idle Feet are chain'd,
  With Frost his Tresses shine.

On yonder Hills that bound our sight
  Already lies the Snow;
Their sides, long streaks of dazzling white
  Amidst their Azure show.
Thy Trees, Kyrle, favourite of the Muse,
  Bare, bleak and naked stand;
No pleasing Spots, no charming views,
  Thy Prospect can command.

'Tis Cold and melancholy all,
  'Tis Dreary to the Eye,
And with Old *Wilton*'s warlike wall
  In Ruins seems to lye.
What now, *Lucinda*, Life inspires?
  What now can make us gay?
Thy Look, our Breasts, *Lucinda*, fires –
  Thy Look creates a May.

But Oh, when Age, Life's winter comes,
  What then, my Fair One, say,
What Wit, Art, Object, Pow'r or Sums,
  What then will make us gay?
Virtue, the Charmer sweet replies,
  Will soften Age's brow –
Virtue, though Wit or Beauty flies,
  Will make us gay as now.

43

Allan Macdougall,
*Winter in the
Olchon Valley*

ALEXANDER POPE

The Man of Ross

Extract from 'Epistle III to Allen Lord Bathurst, of the use of Riches'

Pope:
. . . But all our praises why should lords engross?
Rise, honest Muse! And sing the Man of Ross:
Pleased Vaga echoes through her winding bounds,
And rapid Severn hoarse applause resounds.
Who hung with woods yon mountain's sultry brow?
From the dry rock who bade the waters flow?
Not to the skies in useless columns toss'd,
Or in proud falls magnificently lost,
But clear and artless, pouring through the plain
Health to the sick, and solace to the swain.
Whose causeway parts the vale with shady rows?
Whose seats the weary traveller repose?
Who taught that heaven-directed spire to rise?
'The Man of Ross,' each lisping babe replies.
Behold the market-place with poor o'erspread!
The Man of Ross divides the weekly bread:
He feeds yon almshouse, neat, but void of state,
Where Age and Want sit smiling at the gate
Him portion'd maids, apprenticed orphans bless'd,
The young who labour, and the old who rest.
Is any sick? The Man of Ross relieves,
Prescribes, attends, the medicine makes, and gives.
Is there a variance? Enter but his door,
Balked are the courts, and contest is no more.

Despairing quacks with curses fled the place,
And vile attorneys, now a useless race.
Bathurst:
Thrice happy man! Enabled to pursue
What all so wish, but want the power to do!
Oh say, what sums that generous hand supply?
What mines to swell that boundless charity?
Pope:
Of debts and taxes, wife and children clear,
This man possessed – five hundred pounds a year!
Blush, Grandeur, blush! Proud courts, withdraw your blaze!
Ye little stars, hide your diminish'd rays.
Bathurst:
And what? No monument, inscription, stone?
His race, his form, his name almost unknown?
Pope:
Who builds a church to God, and not to fame,
Will never mark the marble with his name.
Go, search it there, where to be born, and die
Of rich and poor makes all the history;
Enough that Virtue fill'd the space between;
Proved by ends of being, to have been.

Vaga   the River Wye

John Kyrle (1637-1724), the 'Man of Ross', was Oxford educated but lived frugally overlooking Ross's market square. Generous to the young, to the poor, and to Ross church, he established 'The Prospect', a public tree-lined garden-walk. Pope recalls Kyrle's other acts of charity to the town of Ross. This verse-letter from Alexander Pope to Allen, Lord Bathurst (1684-1775), Privy Councillor and patron of poets, recalling Kyrle's acts of charity to the town of Ross, is courteous, teasing and pointed. It was published in *Moral Essays (Epistle III)*. Bathurst, who had a fortune, was establishing a mansion and garden at Cirencester Park.

Left: Cornelius Varley, *The Market Place, Ross*, 1803 (Victoria and Albert Museum)

Right: after Peter Lely, *John Kyrle* (private collection)

46

George Robert
Lewis, *Hereford,
Dynedor and the
Malvern Hills
from the
Haywood Lodge*,
1815
(Tate Gallery)

Epistle to Robert Earl of Oxford and Lord Mortimer (1718)

Alexander
Pope

Such were the notes thy once-loved Poet sung
Till Death untimely stopp'd his tuneful tongue.
Oh just beheld and lost! Admired and mourn'd!
With softest manners, gentlest parts adorn'd!
Blest in each science, blest in ev'ry strain!
Dear to the Muse! To HARLEY dear – in vain!

For him, thou oft hast bid the world attend,
Fond to forget the statesman in the friend;
For SWIFT and him, despised the farce of state,
The sober follies of the wise and great;
Dext'rous, the craving, fawning crowd to quit,
And pleased to 'scape from Flattery to Wit.

Absent or dead, still let a friend be dear,
(A sigh the absent claims, the dead a tear.)
Recall those nights that closed thy toilsome days,
Still hear thy Parnell in his living lays,
Who, careless now of Int'rest, Fame, or Fate,
Perhaps forgets that OXFORD e'er was great;
Or deeming meanest what we greatest call,
Beholds thee glorious only in thy fall.
And sure, if aught below the seats divine
Can touch Immortals, 'tis a soul like thine:
A soul supreme, in each hard instance tried,
Above all pain, all passion, and all pride,
The rage of power, the blast of public breath,
The lust of lucre, and the dread of death.

In vain to deserts thy retreat is made;
The muse attends thee to thy silent shade:
'Tis hers, the brave man's latest steps to trace,
Rejudge his acts, and dignify disgrace.
When Interest calls off all her sneaking train,
And all th'obliged desert, and all the vain;
She waits, or to the scaffold, or the cell,
When the last lingering friend has bid farewell.
Ev'n now, she shades thy evening-walk with bays,
(No hireling she, no prostitute to praise,)
Ev'n now, observant of the parting ray,
Eyes the calm sunset of thy various day,
Through Fortune's cloud one truly great can see,
Nor fears to tell, that MORTIMER is he.

In 1714, a bitter Whig Parliament charged that Robert Harley had secretly negotiated with the French to achieve the Peace of Utrecht. He was confined in the Tower for 18 months and then retired to Brampton Bryan and Eywood. To Harley in this 'desert' Pope addresses an epistle, comforting and admiring. Harley had been amongst men of wit and fashion in the Scriblerus Club; Jonathan Swift, Alexander Pope, John Gay, Dr John Arbuthnot and Thomas Parnell. However, the Club hardly survived Harley's 'Fall'. Parnell (1679-1718) had died. He had been an Irish poet and clergyman (latterly archdeacon) who frequently visited London. 'A Night-Piece on Death', Parnell's poem, prefaced Pope's epistle, so Pope begins: 'Such were the notes . . .' In his *Lives of the Poets* Dr Johnson remarks of Parnell 'that in his latter life he was too much a lover of the bottle, is not denied, but I have heard it imputed to a cause more likely to obtain forgiveness from mankind, the ultimate death of a darling son; or, as others tell, the loss of his wife, who died (1712) in the midst of his expectations.' In the first half of the verse-epistle Pope writes of Parnell, in the second of Harley.

47

JOHN DYER

from The Fleece, *a long poem that celebrates sheep and shepherds*

Pleasant Siluria Book 1 pages 54-6

On spacious airy downs, and gentle hills,
With grass and thyme o'erspread, and clover wild,
Where smiling PHOEBUS tempers ev'ry breeze,
The fairest flocks rejoice! . . .

            . . . such the spacious plain
Of Sarum, spread like ocean's boundless round,
Where solitary Stonehenge, grey with moss,
Ruin of ages, nods: such too the leas
And ruddy tilth, which spiry Ross beholds,
From a green hiloc, o'er her lofty elms;
And Lemster's brooky tract, and airy Croft;
And such Harleian Eywood's swelling turf,
Wav'd as the billows of a rolling sea:
And Shobden, for its lofty terrace fam'd,
Which from a mountain's ridge, elate o'er woods,
And girt with all Siluria, sees around
Regions on regions blended in the clouds.
Pleasant Siluria, land of various views,
Hills, rivers, woods, and lawns, and purple groves
Pomaceous, mingled with the curling growth
Of tendril hops, that flaunt upon their poles,
More airy wild than vines along the sides
Of treacherous Falernum.

Dyer's footnotes: Croft, a seat of Sir Archer Croft; Eywood, of the Earl of Oxford; Shobden, of Lord Bateman; Siluria, the part of England which lies west of the Severn, viz. Herefordshire, Monmouthshire, &c.

Welsh and Silurian Sheep Book 1 pages 60-5

Ye shepherds, if your labors hope success,
Be first your purpose to procure a breed,
To soil and clime adapted. Ev'ry soil
And clime, ev'n ev'ry tree and herb, receives
Its habitant peculiar. . .
Snowden and blue Plynlymmon, and the wide
Aerial sides of Cader-yddris huge;
These are bestow'd on goat-horn'd sheep, of fleece
Hairy and coarse, of long and nimble shank,
Who rove o'er bog or heath, and graze or brouze
Alternate, to collect, with due dispatch,
O'er the bleak wild, the thinly scattered meal.
But hills of milder air, that gently rise
O'er dewy dales, a fairer species boast,
Of shorter limb, and frontlet more ornate;
Such the Silurian. If thy farm extends
Near Cotswold downs, or the delicious groves
Of Symmonds, honour'd through the sandy soil
Of elmy Ross, or Devon's myrtle vales,
That drink clear rivers near the glassy sea;
Regard this sort, and hence the sire of lambs
Select: his tawny fleece in ringlets curls;
Long swings his slender tail; his front is fenc'd
With horns Ammonian, circulating twice
Around each open ear, like those fair scrolls
That grace the columns of th'Ionic dome.

49

James Ward,
*Ryelands Sheep:
the King's Ram,
the King's Ewe
and
Lord Somerville's
Wether,*
1801-07
(Yale Center
for British Art)

The indulgent clime   Book 1 pages 55-6

With grateful heart, ye British swains, enjoy
Your gentle seasons and indulgent clime . . .
. . . Happy at your ease, behold your sheep
Feed on the open turf, or croud the tilth,
Where thick among the greens, with busy mouths
They scoop white turnips: little care is yours;
Only, at morning hour, to interpose
Dry food of oats, or hay, or brittle straw,
The watry juices of the bossy root
Absorbing: or from noxious air to screen
Your heavy teeming ewes, with wattled fence
Of furze or copse-wood, in the lofty field,
Which bleak ascends among the whistling winds.
Or if your sheep are of Silurian breed,
Nightly to house them dry on fern or straw,
Silk'ning their fleeces. Ye, nor rolling hut,
Nor watchful dog, require; where never roar
Of savage tears the air, where careless night
In balmy sleep lies lull'd, and only wakes
To plenteous peace.

50

Shearing festivities   Book 1 pages 81-2

At shearing-time, along the lively vales,
Rural festivities are often heard:
Beneath each blooming arbor all is joy
And lusty merriment: while on the grass
The mingled youth in gaudy circles sport,
We think the golden age again return'd,
And all the fabled Dryades in dance.
Leering they bound along, with laughing air,
To the shrill pipe, and deep remurm'ring chords
Of th'ancient harp, or tabor's hollow sound.

   While the old apart, upon a bank reclin'd,
Attend the tuneful carol, softly mixt
With ev'ry murmur of the sliding wave,
And ev'ry warble of the feather'd choir;
Music of paradise! which still is heard,
When the heart listens; still the views appear
Of the first happy garden, when content
To nature's flow'ry scenes directs the sight.
Yet we abandon those Elysian walks,
Then idly for the lost delight repine:
As greedy mariners, whose desp'rate sails
Skim o'er the billows of the foamy flood,
Fancy they see the less'ning shores retire,
And sigh a farewell to the sinking hills.

   Could I recall those notes, which once the muse
Heard at a shearing . . .

51

George Robert
Lewis,
*Hereford
from the
Haywood, noon,*
1815
(Tate Gallery)

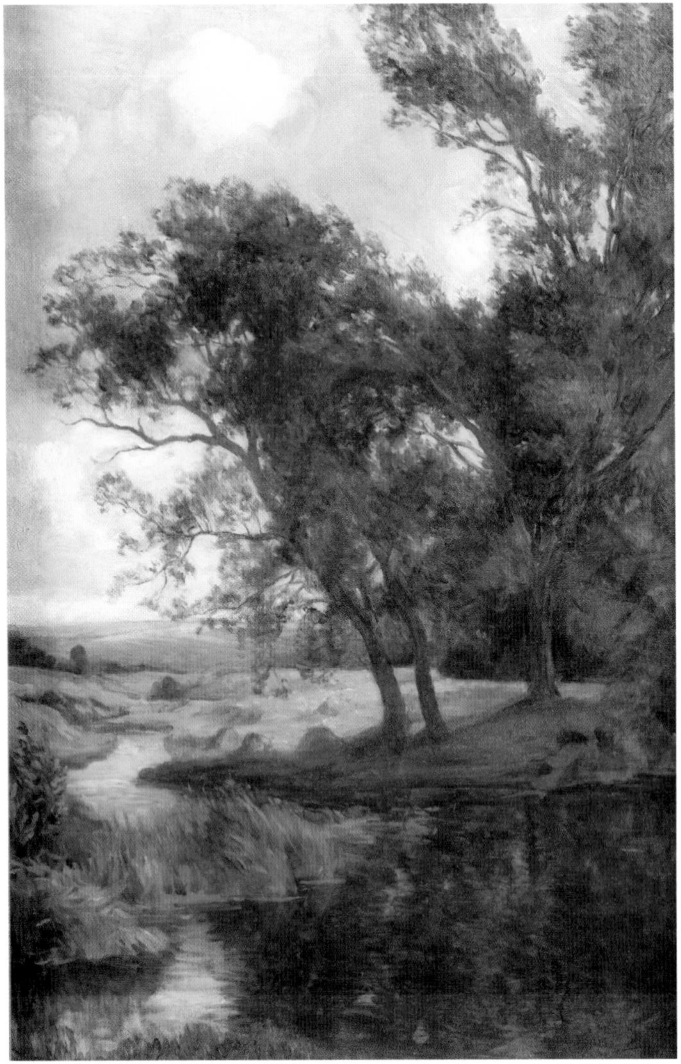

Brian Hatton,
Trees,
Lugg Meadows,
1910
(Hereford
Art Gallery)

The Harley Manuscript

Verses on the planting of five trees at Berrington Castle in the County of Hereford November 15th 1775

41
Verses on the planting of five trees at Berrington Castle
the County of Hereford — Nov.r 15.th 1775

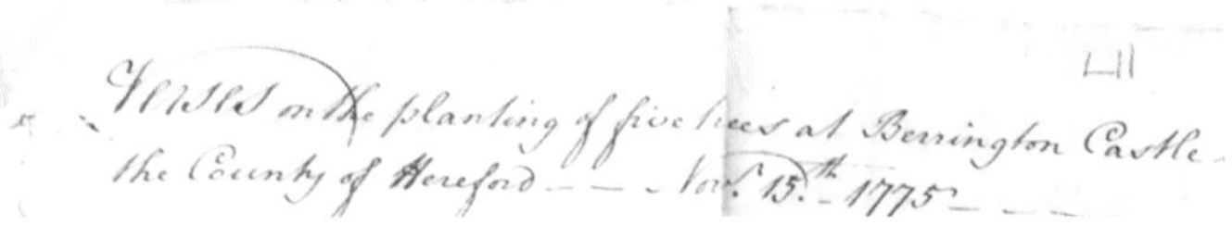

In 1775 the Rt Hon Thomas Harley, banker, MP, former Lord Mayor of London (1768), engaged Lancelot 'Capability' Brown to design his park at Berrington. Brown straightaway planted clusters of trees; the mansion was built later. 'To all conspicuous long these trees shall stand' expresses Capability's insight into how the remodelled landscape would look in years to come. Berrington was Brown's last landscape design. Thomas Harley's only son had died. Of his daughters, Ann, the second, would marry George, son of Admiral Lord Rodney. Thomas Harley later settled Berrington on Ann's second son.

Edward Harley DL of Brampton Bryan Court kindly provided this manuscript. He is doubly connected with Berrington, for his great-grandfather married the daughter of the 6th Lord Rodney. The poem is unsigned. Who was the gracious poet? Was he a member of the Harley family? Was he a friend? Or was he Capability himself?

Stranger behold this little beachen Grove
The seat of Beauty Innocence and Love,
Where planted by the Virgin Sisters five,
The Trees in full Luxuriance long shall thrive;
As when black Clouds the wintry skies deform,
Knit in close Union they defy the Storm,
Repell the Northern Blast, the Eastern Blight,
And all the Horrors of the howling Night.
So shall the Sisters whom Affection binds,
Withstand the Storm of Fate and adverse Winds,
And to the giddy World triumphant prove
The conquering Power of Harmony and Love.
But soon our Summers Sun, and sultry heat
Prompt to the shady Grove and cool Retreat,
Here the fond five their willing Steps shall bend,
And each shall find her tree a sheltering Friend.
  First of the Train see *Martha* gay and fair,
With Hebe's Bloom and lovely flowing Hair,
For whom the Graces all their Power have join'd
To form her Person and adorn her Mind:
Easy, ingaging, elegant and free,
A fund of happy Wit and Pleasantry.
  Nor yet with less delight the Muse shall scan
The soft Perfections of the virtuous *Ann*;
Whose eyes with native Innocence impart
The sweet Effusions of her cheerful Heart.
While Sense, Good-nature, Beauty, Freedom, Ease
Conspire at once to captivate and please,
With loveliest Features that the Face adorn,
With Smiles more cheering than the rosy Morn.

Stranger behold this little beachen Grove.
The Seat of Beauty Innocence and Love.
Where planted by the Virgin Sisters five.
The Trees in full Luxuriance long shall thrive;
As when black Clouds the wintry skies deform,
Knit in close Union they defy the Storm,
Repell the Northern Blast, the Eastern Blight.
And all the Horrors of the howling Night.
So shall the Sisters whom Affection binds,
Withstand the Storm of Fate and adverse Winds,
And to the giddy World triumphant prove
The conquering Power of Harmony and Love.
But soon our Summers Sun, and sultry heat
Prompt to the shady Grove and cool Retreat,
Here the fond five their willing Steps shall bend,
And each shall find her tree a sheltering Friend.
  First of the Train see Martha gay and fair,
With Hebe's Bloom and lovely flowing Hair,
For whom the Graces all their Power have join'd
To form her Person and adorn her Mind:
Easy, engaging, elegant and free,
A Fund of happy Wit and Pleasantry.
  Nor yet with less delight the Muse shall scan
The soft Perfections of the virtuous Ann:
Whose Eyes with native Innocence impart
The sweet Effusions of her cheerful Heart.
While Sense, Good-nature, Beauty, Freedom, Ease,
Conspire at once to captivate and please,
With loveliest Features that the Face adorn,
With Smiles more cheering than the rosy Morn.

See *Sarah* next – observe her graceful Mien
And Elegance of Form like Beauty's Queen,
While modest Diffidence, devoid of Pride,
Hightens each Charm it vainly strives to hide.
  Nor shall the Muse neglect to lend her Aid
To paint the Blushes which the Cheeks o'erspread
Of sweet *Elizabeth* so young, so fair
But she shall be the Muses' future Care,
A tender Bud which Time shall soon disclose,
And give new beauties to the opening Rose.
  Last of the Fair the happy *Margaret* see,
The laughter-loving Maiden, full Glee,
In whom well-pleased we mark the generous Aim
To emulate her older Sister's Fame
Her sweet Good-humour, lively turn, we trace
And catch a glimpse of Martha's Air and Grace.
  Such are the Sisters five the Country's Pride,
Such is the Grove where Peace and Love reside.
And when you see their tow'ring heads appear,
And where the Brecon Mountains black and drear
With awful Grandeur terminate the scene,
Thro' all the expanded Vale that lies between;
To all around (whatever be their Lot
The lofty Castle or the lonely Cot,)
To all conspicuous long these Trees shall stand
A graceful emblem of the Kindred Band,
To future Ages shall extend their Fame,
And *the five happy Sisters* be their name.

George Robert
Lewis,
*Harvest Field
with Reapers,
Haywood,
Herefordshire,*
1815
(Tate Gallery)

Richard Payne Knight

The Landscape
A Didactic Poem in three books, addressed to Uvedale Price, esq (1794)

Richard Payne Knight addressed his poem to Uvedale Price (1747-1829) of Foxley. Knight and Price together promoted the appreciation of the picturesque, so they deplored the schemes of 'Capability' Brown which, Knight held, scraped away local distinctiveness. In 1794 Price published his Essay on the Picturesque, as compared with the Sublime and The Beautiful. *Knight and Price were at the heart of the 'Picturesque debate' of the 1790s. The extracts here reveal Richard Payne Knight's taste for modest, graceful landscape beauty. Uvedale Price in later life corresponded with Elizabeth Barrett Browning.*

How best to bid the verdant Landscape rise
To please the fancy, and delight the eyes,
Its various parts in harmony to join
With art clandestine, and conceal'd design;
To adorn, arrange – to separate and select
With secret skill, and counterfeit neglect –
        I sing.

Do thou, O Price, the song attend,
Instruct the poet, and assist the friend;
Teach him plain truth in numbers to express,
And shew its charms through fiction's flowery dress. . .

. . . Whether the scene extends o'er wide domains,
Or lurks, confined, in low sequester'd plains;
Whether it decks the baron's gorgeous seat,
Or humbly cheers the rustic's snug retreat;
Whether it shews, from yon' high mountain's brow,
The water'd meads and fertile fields below;
Or deep retired in solitude and shade
It bounds its prospect to some narrow glade;

Whether it leads aloft the aching sight
To view the craggy cliff's tremendous height;
Or by the murmuring rivulet's shady side
Delights to shew the curling waters glide
Beneath reflected rocks, or antique towers,
Amidst o'ershadowing trees, or lightly tufted flowers. . .

. . .'Tis still one principle through all extends,
And leads through different ways to different ends.
Whate'er its essence, or whate'er its name,
Whate'er its modes, 'tis still in all the same:
'Tis just congruity of parts combined
To please the sense, and satisfy the mind.
In form of limb and character of face,
We call the magic combination *grace;*
That *grace* which springs from an unfetter'd mind,
Which rules the body, free and unconfined . . .
The best approach to every beauteous scene
Is where it's least expected or forseen;
Where naught occurs to anticipate surprise,
Or bring the Landscape piecemeal to the eyes . . .

Thomas
Gainsborough,
*Beech Trees
at Foxley,
Herefordshire,
with Yazor
Church in the
Distance*, 1760
(Whitworth
Gallery,
Manchester)

Anthony Devis, *Foxley*, undated (Hereford Art Gallery)

58

Cautiously will *taste* its stores reveal;
Its greatest art is aptly to conceal –
To lead, with secret guile, the prying sight
To where component parts may best unite
And form one beauteous, nicely blended whole,
To charm the eye and captivate the soul. . .

. . . Well mix'd and blended in the scene, you shew
The stately mansion rising to the view.

But mix'd and blended, ever let it be
A mere component part of what you see.
For if in solitary pride it stand
'Tis but a lump, encumbering the land,
A load if inert matter, cold and dead,
Th'excrescence of the lawns that round it spread.
Component parts in all the eye requires;
One formal mass for ever palls and tires.
To make the landscape graceful to the sight
Three points of distance ever should unite . . .

WILLIAM WORDSWORTH

Lines Composed a Few Miles above Tintern Abbey,
on Revisiting the Banks of the Wye during a Tour, July 13th 1798

Five years have passed; five summers, with the length
Of five long winters! And again I hear
These waters, rolling from their mountain-springs
With a soft inland murmur. – Once again
Do I behold these steep and lofty cliffs,
That on a wild secluded scene impress
Thoughts of a more deep seclusion; and connect
The landscape with the quiet of the sky.
The day is come when I again repose
Here, under this dark sycamore, and view
These plots of cottage-ground, these orchard-tufts,
Which at this season, with their unripe fruits,
Are clad in one green hue, and lose themselves
'Mid groves and copses. Once again I see
These hedge-rows, hardly hedge-rows, little lines
Of sportive wood run wild: those pastoral farms,
Green to the very door; and wreathes of smoke
Sent up, in silence, from among the trees!
With some uncertain notice, as might seem
Of vagrant dwellers in the houseless woods,
Or of some Hermit's cave, where by his fire
The Hermit sits alone.
                                    These beauteous forms,
Through a long absence, have not been to me
As is a landscape to a blind man's eye:
But oft, in lonely rooms, and 'mid the din
Of towns and cities, I have owed to them

In hours of weariness, sensations sweet,
Felt in the blood, and felt along the heart;
And passing even into my purer mind,
With tranquil restoration: – feelings too
Of unremembered pleasure: such, perhaps,
As have no slight or trivial influence
On that best portion of a good man's life,
His little, nameless, unremembered acts
Of kindness and of love. Nor less, I trust,
To them I may have owed another gift,
Of aspect more sublime; that blessed mood,
In which the burden of the mystery,
In which the heavy and the weary weight
Of this unintelligible world,
Is lightened: – that serene and blessed mood,
In which the affections gently lead us on, –
Until, the breath of this corporeal frame
And even the motion of our human blood
Almost suspended, we are laid asleep
In body, and become a living soul:
While with an eye made quiet by the power
Of harmony, and the deep power of joy,
We see into the life of things.
                                                If this
Be but a vain belief, yet, oh! How oft –
In darkness and amid the many shapes
Of joyless daylight; when the fretful stir

Samuel Palmer,
Tintern Abbey at Sunset, 1861
(Yale Center for British Art)

Unprofitable, and the fever of the world,
Have hung upon the beatings of my heart –
How oft, in spirit, have I turned to thee,
O sylvan Wye! Thou wanderer thro’ the woods,
How often has my spirit turned to thee!

   And now, with gleams of half-extinguished thought,
With many recognitions dim and faint,
And somewhat of a sad perplexity,
The picture of the mind revives again:
While here I stand, not only with the sense
Of present pleasure, but with the pleasing thoughts
That in this moment there is life and food
For future years. And so I dare to hope,
Though changed, no doubt, from what I was when first
I came among these hills; when like a roe
I bounded o’er the mountains, by the sides
Of the deep rivers, and the lonely streams,
Wherever nature led: more like a man
Flying from something that he dreads, than one
Who sought the thing he loved. For nature then
(the coarser pleasures of my boyish days,
And their glad animal movements all gone by)
To me was all in all. – I cannot paint
What then I was. The sounding cataract
Haunted me like a passion: the tall rock,
The mountain, and the deep and gloomy wood,
Their colours and their forms, were then to me
An appetite; a feeling and a love,
That had no need of a remoter charm,

By thought supplied, nor any interest
Unborrowed from the eye. – That time is past,
And all its aching joys are now no more,
And all its dizzy raptures. Not for this
Faint I, nor mourn nor murmur; other gifts
Have followed; for such loss, I would believe,
Abundant recompense. For I have learned
To look on nature, not as in the hour
Of thoughtless youth; but hearing oftentimes,
The still, sad music of humanity,
Nor harsh, nor grating, though of ample power
To chasten and subdue. And I have felt
A presence that disturbs me with the joy
Of elevated thoughts; a sense sublime
Of something far more deeply interfused,
Whose dwelling is the light of setting suns,
And the round ocean and the living air,
And the blue sky, and in the mind of man;
A motion and a spirit, that impels
All thinking things, all objects of all thought,
And rolls through all things. Therefore am I still
A lover of the meadows and the woods,
And mountains; and of all that we behold
From this green earth; of all the mighty world
Of eye and ear, – both what they half create,
And what perceive; well pleased to recognise
In nature and the language of the sense,
The anchor of my purest thoughts, the nurse
The guide, the guardian of my heart, and soul
Of all my moral being.

62

Samuel Palmer,
*Tintern Abbey
from near the
Chepstow Road,
looking towards
Monmouth*, c.1835
(Fitzwilliam
Museum,
Cambridge)

We are Seven

William Wordsworth

William Wordsworth conversed with the little Maid near the ruins of Goodrich Castle in October 1793.
In 1798 his friend Samuel Coleridge wrote versions of the initial verses; Wordsworth and he were then
collaborating on The Ancient Mariner, *a poem in similar metre.* We are Seven *was published in their* Lyrical Ballads *of 1798.*

A simple Child,
That lightly draws its breath,
And feels its life in every limb,
What should it know of death?

I met a little cottage Girl:
She was eight years old, she said;
Her hair was thick with many a curl
That clustered round her head.

She had a rustic, woodland air,
And she was wildly clad:
Her eyes were fair, and very fair;
Her beauty made me glad.

'Sisters and brothers, little Maid,
How many may you be?'
'How many? Seven in all,' she said,
And wondering looked at me.

'And where are they? I pray you tell.'
She answered, 'Seven are we;
And two of us at Conway dwell,
And two are gone to sea.

'Two of us in the churchyard lie,
My sister and my brother;

And in the churchyard cottage, I
Dwell near them with my mother.'

'You say that two at Conway dwell,
And two are gone to sea,
Yet you are seven! – I pray you tell,
Sweet Maid, how this may be?'

Then did the little Maid reply,
'Seven boys and girls are we;
Two of us in the churchyard lie,
Beneath the churchyard tree,'

'You run about, my little Maid,
Your limbs they are alive;
If two are in the churchyard laid,
Then you are only five.'

'Their graves are green, they may be seen,'
The little Maid replied,
'Twelve steps or more from my mother's door,
And they are side by side.

'My stockings there I often knit,
My kerchief there I hem;
And there upon the ground I sit,
And sing a song to them.

William Wordsworth

'And often after sunset, Sir,
When it is light and fair,
I take my little porringer,
And eat my supper there.

'The first that died was little Jane;
In bed she moaning lay,
Till God released her of her pain,
And then she went away.

So in the churchyard she was laid;
And all the summer dry,
Together round her grave we played,
My brother John and I.

'And when the ground was white with snow,
And I could run and slide,
My brother John was forced to go,
And he lies by her side.'

'How many are you, then,' said I,
'If they two are in Heaven?'
The little Maiden did reply.
'O Master! we are seven.'

'But they are dead; those two are dead!
Their spirits are in Heaven!'
'Twas throwing words away: for still
The little Maid would have her will,
And said, 'Nay, we are seven!'

64

Charles F. Walker,
Goodrich Church
(Herefordshire
Libraries)

ROBERT BLOOMFIELD

The Banks of the Wye (1811)

Robert Bloomfield prefaced his 49 page poem: 'In the summer of 1807, a party of my good friends in Gloucestershire proposed to themselves a short excursion down the Wye, and through part of South Wales. . . . Should the reader, from being a resident, or frequent visitor, be well acquainted with the route, and able to discover inaccuracies in distances, succession of objects, or local particulars, he is requested to recollect, that the party was out but ten days; a period much too short for correct and laborious description, but quite sufficient for all the powers of poetry which I feel capable of exerting. The whole exhibits the language and feelings of a man who had never before seen a mountainous country; and of this it is highly necessary that the reader should be apprized.'

. . . Ross, that exalts its spire on high,
Above the flow'ry-margin'd WYE,
Scene of the morrow's joy, that prest
Its unseen beauties on our rest
In dreams; but who of dreams would tell,
Where truth sustains the song so well?

The morrow came, and Beauty's eye
Ne'er beamed upon a lovlier sky;
Imagination instant brought,
And dash'd, amidst the train of thought,
Tints of the bow. The boatman stript;
Glee at the helm exulting tript,
And wav'd her flower-encircled wand,
'Away, away, to Fairy Land.'

Light dipped the oars; but who can name
The various objects dear to fame,
That changing, doubling, wild, and strong,
Demand the noblest powers of song?

Awhile the grazing herd was seen,
And trembling willow's silver green,
Till the fantastic current stood
In line direct for PENCRAIG WOOD;
Whose bold green summit welcome bade,
Then rear'd behind his nodding shade.
Here, as the light boat skimm'd along,
The clarionet, and chosen song,
That mellow, wild, Eolian lay,
'Sweet in the Woodlands,' roll'd away
In echoes down the stream, that bore
Each dying clause to every shore
And forward Cape, and woody range,
That form the never-ceasing change
To him who floating, void of care,
Twirls with the stream, he knows not where;
Till bold, impressive, and sublime,
Gleam'd all that's left by storms and time
Of GOODRICH TOWERS. The mould'ring pile
Tells noble truths, – but dies the while;

Joshua Cristall,
*Monnow Bridge
at Monmouth*,
1803
(Tate Gallery)

O'er the steep path, through brake and briar,
His batter'd turrets still aspire,
In rude magnificence. 'Twas here
LANCASTRIAN HENRY spread his cheer
When came the news that HAL was born,
And MONMOUTH hail'd th'auspicious morn;
A boy in sports, a prince in war,
Wisdom and valour crowned his car;
Of France the terror, England's glory,
As Stratford's bard has told the story . . .

. . . 'Here kings shall dwell,' the builders cried;
'Here England's foes shall low'r their pride;
Hither shall suppliant nobles come,
And this be England's royal home.'
Vain hope! For on the Gwentian shore
The regal banner streams no more!
Nettles, and vilest weeds that grow
To mock poor grandeur's head laid low,
Creep round the turrets valour rais'd,
And flaunt where youth and beauty gaz'd.

Here fain would strangers loiter long,
And muse as Fancy's woof grows strong;
Yet cold the heart that could complain,
Where POLLETT struck his oars again;
For lovely as the sleeping child,
The stream glides on sublimely wild,
In perfect beauty, perfect ease;
The awning trembled in the breeze,

67

Nicholas Pocock,
*Wye Tour Boat
Passing Welsh
Newton*, 1791
(Norwich Castle
Museum)

And scarcely trembled, as we stood
For RUERDEAN Spire, and BISHOP'S WOOD.
The fair domains of COURTFIELD made
A paradise of mingled shade
Round BICKNOR'S tiny church, that cowers
Beneath his host of woodland bowers.

But who the charm of words shall fling,
O'er RAVEN CLIFF and COLDWALL Spring,
To brighten the unconscious eye,
And wake the soul to ecstasy?

Noon scorch'd the fields; the boat lay to;
The dripping oars had nought to do,
Where round us rose a scene that might
Enchant an idiot – glorious sight!
Here, in one gay according mind,
Upon the sparkling stream we din'd;
As shepherds free on mountain heath,
Free as the fish that watch'd beneath
For falling crumbs, where cooling lay
The wine that cheered us on our way.
Th'unruffled bosom of the stream
Gave every tint and every gleam;

Gave shadowy rocks, and clear blue sky,
And double clouds of various dye;
Gave dark green woods, or russet brown,
And pendant corn-fields, upside down.

A troop of gleaners chang'd their shade,
And 'twas a change by music made;
For slowly to the bank they drew,
To mark our joy, and share it too.
How oft, in childhood's flow'ry days,
I've heard the wild impassion'd lays
Of such a group, lays strange and new,
And thought, was ever song so true?
When from the hazel's cool retreat,
They watched the summer's trembling heat;
And through the boughs rude urchins play'd'
Where matrons, round the laughing maid,
Prest the long grass beneath! And here
They doubtless shar'd an equal cheer;
Enjoy'd the feast with equal glee,
And rais'd the song of revelry:
Yet half abash'd reserv'd, and shy,
Watch'd till the strangers glided by.

Pollett the boatman (Bloomfield's footnote)

69

Brian Hatton,
*The Waggon,
Warham,
with Jones
the Waggoner,*
1909
(Hereford
Art Gallery)

ELIZABETH BARRETT BROWNING

from Aurora Leigh (1856)

Early in EBB's verse-novel, Aurora tells how she learnt to love the countryside. From the grand home of a moralistic aunt she had at times escaped to the Malvern hills and valleys. Later she had walked out with Romney, a charming, conscience-driven friend.

I learnt to love that England. Very oft,
Before the day was born, or otherwise
Through secret windings of the afternoons
I threw my hunters off and plunged myself
Among the deep hills, as a hunted stag
Will take the waters, shivering with the fear
And passion of the course. And when at last
Escaped, so many a green slope built on slope
Betwixt me and the enemy's house behind,
I dared to rest, or wander, in a rest
Made sweeter for the step upon the grass,
And view the ground's most gentle dimplement
(As if God's finger touched but did not press
In making England), such an up and down
Of verdure, – nothing too much up or down,
A ripple of land; such little hills, the sky
Can stoop to tenderly and the wheatfields climb;
Such nooks of valleys lined with orchises,
Fed full of noises by invisible streams;
And open pastures where you scarcely tell
White daisies from white dew, – at intervals
The mythic oaks and elm-trees standing out
Self-poised upon their prodigy of shade, –
I thought my father's land was worthy too
Of being my Shakespeare's.

> Very oft alone,
Unlicensed; not infrequently with leave
To walk the third with Romney and his friend
The rising painter, Vincent Carrington . . .

> Often we walked only two
If cousin Romney pleased to walk with me.
We read, or talked, or quarrelled, as it chanced.
We were not lovers, nor even friends well-matched:
Say rather, scholars upon different tracks,
And thinkers disagreed: he, overfull
Of what is, and I, haply, overbold
For what might be.

> But then the thrushes sang
And shook my pulses and the elms' new leaves;
At which I turned, and held my finger up,
And bade him mark that, howsoe'er the world
Went ill, as he related, certainly
The thrushes still sang in it. At the word
His brow would soften, – and he bore with me
In melancholy patience, not unkind,
While breaking into voluble ecstasy
I flattered all the beauteous country round,
As poets use, the skies, the clouds, the fields,
The happy violets hiding from the roads

The primroses run down to, carrying gold;
The tangled hedgerows, where the cows push out
Impatient horns and tolerant churning mouths
'Twixt dripping ash-boughs, – hedgerows all alive
With birds and gnats and large white butterflies
Which look as if the May-flower had caught life
And palpitated forth upon the wind;
Hills, vales, woods, netted in a silver mist,
Farms, granges, doubled up among the hills;
And cattle grazing in the watered vales,
And cottage-chimneys smoking from the woods,
And cottage-gardens smelling everywhere,
Confused with smell of orchards. 'See,' I said,
'And see! Is God not with us on the earth?' . . .
. . . And ankle-deep in English grass I leaped
And clapped my hands, and called all very fair.

Brian Hatton,
The Skylark, 1906
(Hereford Art Gallery)

Francis Kilvert the diarist

Clyro Water (March 1875)

Oh, Clyro Water! ceaselessly
For seven sweet years my lullaby;
My life, my love, my footsteps free
For seven sweet years have been by thee;
And as life stole from year to year
Thy voice still more I loved to hear,
Whether with storms thy roar was high,
Or when thou softly murmured'st by
With summer nights' melodious tones,
And quiet clink amongst thy stones.
And often I, when sheltered warm,
From driving rain and howling storm,
Have listened from the lighted book
To hear the roaring of the brook;
And as it thundered, rising still,
It brought a message from the hill
Of torrent, rain and tempest still.
But when thy waters dimpling smiled
Adown the Cwm some sweet spring day,
Fern-fringed, flower-lighted on their way

By primrose stars that shone on thee,
And many a wood anemone,
How I have watched on the green breast
Of orchards sloping to the west,
In sister groups about the hills
The yellow-coated daffodils
Through all the bright March afternoon
Dance, nodding to thy rippling tune.
On Sunday morns the church-bells shook
Sweet music o'er the murmuring brook,
That flowed in chime; and from the hill
The parish folk came wending still
Churchwards from many a mountain ridge,
And loitered, leaning on the bridge
To talk, before the dropping chime
Gave warning of the service time;
And ere had ceased the parson's bell,
A silence o'er the village fell,
For all the churchyard path had trod,
And gathering kneeled to worship God,
And the sole sound the air that shook
Was the sweet tinkle of the brook.

Sweet Clyro Water! oh, let me
Still by thy banks remembered be,
And keep yet as thy grasses green,
The love for me that once has been!
And if 'tis given to me once more
To tread thy well-remembered shore,
May I not wander there unknown,
But find a hand to clasp my own,
A voice of welcome, gladdening eyes
And kindly smiles or kindlier sighs.
But, oh, meanwhile, sweet stream, by thee
May many a prayer arise for me,
May kind thoughts, wishes that in heaven
Are counted prayers, at morn and even
From these worn water-steps below
The mountain-ash, still heavenward go
For him who exiled far away
For his dear friends doth ever pray.

Vanessa Pomeroy,
Spring Light,
Yellow Field,
Hay Bluff

74

Luke Piper,
Whitney-on-Wye

New Whitney on Wye   11.XI.08

Paradise, Clyro (28 August 1878)

I met within the village street
A cottage maiden, shy and sweet;
'Whence do you come,' I said, 'fair child?'
'From Paradise,' she said, and smiled.
And as I gazed it seemed to me
How true the simple word might be,
A truth beyond what she could guess
In her sweet unconsciousness,
For there still lingered in her eyes
Gleams from the light of Paradise,
And through her features yet did shine
A likeness of the Face Divine.
Most true the vision that did show
How the blest spirits come and go;
Downward they pass to earth from heaven
To tell how sin may be forgiven.
And heavenward – as with a new birth –
To teach our souls to rise from earth.
From Jacob's Dream thus may we know
Whence we have come and whither go,
To work on earth from morn till even,
Then seek our rest and home in heaven.
Sweet child, when thy life's work is done,
And thou dost sleep at set of sun,
With the blest angels may'st thou rise
From Paradise to Paradise.

Paradise Farm is in the hills above Clyro.

John Masefield

from The Everlasting Mercy (1911)

Saul Kane had lived a wild, oafish life: 'I drank, I fought, I poached, I whored. . .' He had won a bare-knuckle fight in the woods, and in a Ledbury cider-house with rough mates caroused until stupefied. The change within him was first occasioned by the sight and sounds of Ledbury's ancient buildings.

From three long hours of gin and smokes
And two girls' breath and fifteen blokes,
A warmish night, and windows shut,
The room stank like a fox's gut.
The heat and smell and drinking deep
Began to stun the gang to sleep.
Some fell downstairs to sleep on the mat,
Some snored it sodden where they sat.
Dick Twot had lost a tooth and wept,
But all the drunken others slept.
Jane slept beside me in the chair,
And I got up; I wanted air.

I opened the window wide and leaned
Out of that pigstye of the fiend
And felt a cool wind go like grace
About the sleeping market-place.
The clock struck three, and sweetly, slowly,
The bells chimed Holy, Holy, Holy;
And in a second's pause there fell
The cold note of the chapel bell,
And then a cock crew, flapping wings,
And summat made me think of things.

How long those ticking clocks had gone
From church and chapel, on and on,
Ticking the time out, ticking slow
To men and girls who'd come and go,
And how they ticked in belfry dark
When half the town was bishop's park,
And how they'd run a chime full tilt
The night after the church was built,
And how that night was Lambert's Feast,
The night I'd fought and been a beast.
And how a change had come. And then
I thought, 'You tick to different men.'
What with the fight and what with drinking
And being awake alone there thinking,
My mind began to carp and tetter,
'If this life's all, the beasts are better.'
And then I thought, 'I wish I'd seen
The many towns this town has been;
I wish I knew if they'd a-got
A kind of summat we've a-not,
If them as built the church so fair
Were half the chaps folk say they were;

Anonymous
artist,
*Ledbury
Looking 'West'
[actually North]*,
c.1820
(Hereford
Art Gallery)

John Masefield

For they'd the skill to draw their plan,
And skill's a joy to any man:
And they'd the strength, not skill alone,
To build it beautiful in stone;
And strength and skill together thus . . .
O, they were happier men than us.

But if they were, they had to die
The same as every one and I.
And no one lives again, but dies,
And all the bright goes out of eyes,
And all the skill goes out of hands,
And all the wise brain understands,
And all the beauty, all the power

Is cut down like a withered flower.
In all the show from birth to rest
I give the poor dumb cattle best.'

I wondered, then, why life should be,
And what would be the end of me
When youth and health and strength were gone
And cold old age came creeping on?
A keeper's gun? The Union ward?
Or that new quod at Hereford?
And looking round I felt disgust
At all the nights of drink and lust,
And all the looks of all the swine
Who'd said that they were friends of mine . . .

Brian Hatton,
*Counting
the Sheep*,
1900
(Hereford
Art Gallery)

Edmund
Ward Gill,
Hereford Cow,
undated
(Hereford
Art Gallery)

80

G.R. Lewis,
*Agricultural
workers*, 1815
(Victoria and
Albert Museum)

E.V. Knox (Evoe)

Hell in Herefordshire (1911)

E.V. Knox (1881-1971), editor of Punch *from 1932 to 1949, was one of four brothers and two sisters, divergent and brilliantly witty, Msg. Ronnie Knox among them. E.V. penned topical satirical poems under the pseudonym 'Evoe'. In evidence to the Licensing Commission the Bishop of Hereford had stated that there was much 'secret cider-drinking' in his diocese. The diocese of Hereford includes south-west Shropshire.*

The wild white rose is cankered
Along the Vale of Lugg,
There is poison in the tankard,
There's murder in the mug;

Through all the pleasant valleys
Where stand the palefaced kine
Men raise the devil's chalice
And drink his bitter wine.

Unspeakable carouses
That shame the summer sky
Take place in little houses
That look towards the Wye;

And near the Radnor border
And the dark hills of Wales
Beelzebub is warder
And sorcery prevails.

For spite of Church or chapel
Ungodly folk there be
Who pluck the cider apple
From the cider apple tree,

And squeeze it in their presses
Until the juice runs out,
At various addresses
That no one knows about.

And maddened by the orgies
Of that unholy brew
They slit each other's gorges
From one a.m. till two,

Till Ledbury is a shambles
And in the dirt and mud
Where Leominster sits and gambles
The dice are stained with blood.

But still, if strength suffices
Before the day is done,
I'll go and share the vices
Of Clungunford and Clun;

I'll watch the red sun sinking
Across the March again
And join the secret drinking
Of outlaws in Presteigne.

Siegfried Sassoon

At the grave of Henry Vaughan (1927)

Henry Vaughan's grave is in the churchyard of Llansantffraed.

Above the voiceful windings of a river
An old green slab of simply graven stone
Shuns notice, overshadowed by a yew.
Here Vaughan lies dead, whose name flows on for ever
Through pastures of the spirit washed with dew
And starlit with eternities unknown.
Here sleeps the Silurist; the loved physician;
The face that left no portraiture behind;
The skull that housed white angels and had vision
Of daybreak through the gateways of the mind.

Here faith and mercy, wisdom and humility
(Whose influence shall prevail for evermore)
Shine. And this lowly grave tells Heaven's tranquillity.
And here stand I, a suppliant at the door.

83

Edmund
Mariner Gill,
*Mill in Ruins
on the banks
of the River Usk*,
1858
(Hereford
Art Gallery)

ROLAND MATHIAS

Thomas ap Richard of Doier to the Tower, These (1947)

This ballad purports to be a secret letter sent in 1605 to William Morgan of Treville Park in Archenfield, prisoner in the Tower of London, the sender being his Catholic neighbour, Thomas ap Richard (Pritchard) of New Grange. Roland Mathias, historian as well as poet, published in Whitsun Riot *(1963) his research of these events. A 'commotion' occurred because the vicar of Allensmore had refused to bury a Papist's body in his churchyard. In defiance Catholics gathered early one morning near Allensmore church and secretly buried the woman's body. When he learned of this illegality the Bishop of Hereford set off for Archenfield accompanied by armed men led by Sir James Scudamore of Holme Lacy. They intended to seize William Morgan, a Catholic of some standing. To thwart Scudamore and the Bishop, Thomas Pritchard mustered Catholics and prepared an ambush. In the event William Morgan did not resist his own arrest so the planned Catholic ambush fell into disarray. The date of this 'Whitsun Riot' is significant – 21st May to 5th June 1605 – just five months before Guy Fawkes' Plot.*

Evening is grey with us, Morgan,
  Mist on the low ground:
Restless we are as coneys
  Who once slept sound.

Sir Scudamore he took you,
  And the bishop white as his bands:
Our sixty pikes close in the valletts
  Would have served your ends –

But you smiled your wisdom, Morgan,
  And went with them to the Tower.
What devil's sky in London
  Leers us this hour?

The mountains despair for Arkston,
  Grave the mound is with prayers:
The tall wood of Treville
  Hides greater fears.

The grey men in the hamlet,
  The weavers of Hungerstone,
Work looms that events have lately
  High overgrown.

Wormbridge is awed and quiet,
  Quarrell in hiding. O
Where are the swords in earnest
  For one more blow?

We have only the words now, Morgan,
  Weapons are slack in our hands.
We run in this sorry evening
  The bishop's errands.

Vaughan of New Court in the valley
  Reveals his receipt from hell:
If evil befall you, fully
  With book and bell

We'll curse him for your sake, Morgan,
  And the candle save for your mass
Who die that the true faith be preserved
  Fearless for us.

The Bishop Robert Bennett
valletts a wooded dell
Quarrell Thomas Quarrell of Wormbridge, a leader of the planned
  ambush
Vaughan of New Court Rowland Vaughan (the subject of John Davies'
  Panegyricke) supported the Bishop of Hereford. He joined other
  justices and armed men in a search for evidence of Catholic practice. Villagers all along the borders fled. A rumour arose that the
  soldiers beheaded an outlawed priest named Ainsworth.

Craswall (1947)

With a long stirrup under fern
From a small blast of oaks and thorn
The shepherd scours the circling hill
And the sharp dingle creeping to the well.

A trickle from the canting neck
A pony coughing in the track
Are all the stranger hears, and steep
Among the ferns the threading of the sheep.

This is the boundary: different burrs
Stick, stones make darker scars
On the road down: nightingales
Struggle with thorn-trees for the gate of Wales.

85

Canting neck the spring-water's tilted channel
Burrs probably both 'sticky-buds' and 'regional accents'
Craswall is on the border of Wales

Charles F. Walker,
Allensmore Church, 1867
(Herefordshire Libraries)

RONALD JOHNSON

from The Book of the Green Man (1976)

April 8th

We began today
to trace the course
of the Wye

into "Wild
Wales," Chepstow to Plynlimmon –

limestone bed & cliff –

forest & grassy source.

And as I write this, tonight, at St. Briavels
– a castle squat as a toad, with a moat full of primroses –

I invoke the Wye itself
to cut these pages: its Celtic loops & interlacements,

its continuities that lead the view

onward, & back

to Kilvert – Vaughan.

The echoes of its slow rush ever to be
listened for
in Watershed. . .

Greensward & Sheep. . .

O wind your waters through my song, green Wye.

...

The wind off
Wyndcliffe

& the spiraling out of sight

of larks in flight.

O wind your waters through these songs, & mine –

river Wye,

green Wye.

87

Brian Hatton,
*The River Wye
at Sugwas*,
1906
(Hereford
Art Gallery)

88

April 12th

Two days of mossy mists,
soft & clinging. The river, a single grey thread
to be followed through other greys.

Quiet brown blurs
of Hereford cattle, shadowy
swans.

Only the harsh clamor of rooks penetrates.

Though once, a dead sheep floated downstream, every curl,
of its coat, distinct as the bubble

in a house-of-spittle.
Its head like a withered apple.

Today, the Black

Mountains

are a smoke

you could put your hand through

& celandines reflect

the light back like mirrors.

We stopped at Moccas, where Kilvert wrote:

"Those grey
old men of Moccas –

those grey, gnarled, low-browed, knock-kneed,
bowed, bent, huge, strange,
long-armed, deformed, hunch-backed, misshapen oak men –

that stand with both feet in the grave,
yet seeing out,

with such tales to tell,
as when they whisper to each other,
nights,

the silver
birches weep, poplars
& aspens shiver

& long ears of the hares
& rabbits stand

on end."

And a sparkling snow – from somewhere – through sunshine –

appeared

in clear air.

Trevor Makinson,
*March in
Herefordshire*,
1944
(Hereford
Art Gallery)

89

Jacob George
Strutt,
Moccas Oak,
c.1830
(from *Sylva
Britannica*)

The Moccas church of
tufa. North Door carved with a Beast eating

the Tree of Life, & the South*, with Beast seen devouring a man*

who holds the Tree of Life, the branches of which
form a cross.

And close by, Bredwardine, where Kilvert lies buried.

Where from his grave, "bright

shoots":

daffodil, primrose, snow-drop, white violet.

April 13th

Here, the river swept great
curves
along wide valleys.

We left our footprints

green, behind,
as we followed the straight bright dew-path, meadow banks gleaming.

Clouds moved down the valley – their shadows
a river of huge dapples – their glowing masses opening above
as we came,

a white enveloping progression.

April 15th, Easter Sunday

We walked in rain
to Llansantffread

– Vaughan buried at St. Bridgit
(the Saint of Light,

born at sunrise on the first day of spring) on
the Usk (as *Vaughan,*

the Swan of). Inside, a font of yellow

sallow

white iris

& freesia the color of ivory.

". . . With what floures
And shoots of glory, my Soul breaks." "Living bowers."

Silex Scintillans
these mountains –

the Black & Brecon Beacons
– a deep but dazzling darkness. Beckoning. . .

dissolving,

to white cloud

& swan, & clod.

Everything,

one river running. . .

April 19th

Cuckoo. . . cuckoo. . . cuckoo. . .

I had been listening for the first cuckoo, Delius' cuckoo –

but the sound is softer, more penetrant. "Calling

about the hills," Kilvert says. Yes,

it is that. An echo. . . :

this green source, this welling-forth in ever-widening circles,

this "spring".

92

FRANCES HOROVITZ

Rowlestone Haiku

*for the Armstongs of Rowlestone Mill
and the de Waals of Cwm Cottage*

Two snows are falling,
winter's blossom, spring's. One takes
all summer to melt

Lamb or melting snow?
From high fields only shepherds
tell, this wintry spring.

Old Song

Birdsong outside my window
recalls tremblings of water.

I lay alone
deep in ferns by the stream's edge;
only the bees hum
and the labyrinthine murmurings
entered my mind.

Birdsong and water bear away grief.

I walked home through the mountain mist
calling your name.

Brian Hatton,
Ailsa Marr Hatton,
1907
(Hereford
Art Gallery)

Prayer to the Lady of Kilpeck

Lady of confetti and violets

Lady open to all winds

O lady of the stone cleft

Be shining to my lover

As bird or fox

Among these hills.

May he lie by this stone wall

Out of the wind's way.

O lady of the quick snake

May he knock soon

At my seven doors

In the spring grass.

O lady of yew trees

Bright harridan

Be swift

At your last coming.

Evening

Lilac blossom crests the window sill
mingling whiteness with the good dark of this room.
A bloom of light hangs delicately in white painted angles.
Bluebells heaped in a pot
still hold their blue against the dark;
I see their green stalks glisten.

Thin as a swan's bone
I wait for the lessons of pain and light.
Grief is a burden, useless.
It must dissolve into the dark.
I see the hills, luminous.
There will be the holly tree
the hawthorn with mistletoe
foxgloves springing in thousands.

The hills also will pass away
                will remain
as this lilac light, these blue bells,
the good dark of this room.

95

Brian Hatton,
Ailsa Hatton,
1908
(Hereford
Art Gallery)

Kilpeck (1974)

We are dried and brittle this morning,
fragile with continence, quiet.
You have brought me to see a church.
I stare at a Norman arch in red sandstone
carved like a Mayan temple-gate;
at serpents writhing up the doorposts
and squat saints with South-American features
who stare back over our heads
from a panel of beasts and fishes.
　　　The gargoyles jutting from under the eaves
are the colour of newborn children.

Last night you asked me
if poetry was the most important thing.

We walk on around the building
craning our heads back to look up
at lions, griffins, fat-faced bears.
The Victorians broke some of these figures
as being too obscene for a church;
but they missed the Whore of Kilpeck.
She leans out under the roof
holding her pink stony cleft agape
with her ancient little hands.
There was always witchcraft here, you say.

The sheep-track up to the fragments
of castle-wall is fringed with bright bushes.

Sheela-na-gig,
Kilpeck Church

We clamber awkwardly, separate.
Hawthorn and dogrose offer hip and haws,
orange and crimson capsules, pretending
harvest. I taste a blackberry.
The soil here is coloured like brick-dust,
like the warm sandstone. A fruitful county.
We regard it uneasily.

There is little left to say
after all the talk we had last night
instead of going to bed –
fearful for our originality,
avoiding the sweet obvious act
as if it were the only kind of indulgence.
Silly, perhaps.
　　　　　　　We have our reward.
We are languorous now, heavy
with whatever we were conserving,
carrying each a delicate burden
of choices made or about to be made.
Words whisper hopefully in our heads.

Slithering down the track we hold hands
to keep a necessary balance.
The gargoyles extend their feral faces,
rosy, less lined than ours.
We are wearing out our identities.

96

RUTH BIDGOOD

Cwmioie

So hot! Colours are soft in haze,
long tawny grass round the tombs,
brown shoulders of boys and girls
sunning by the crooked church.
Built on tiptilted rock, it leans
every which way, buttressed,
stable after its fashion, with an air
of kindly eccentricity.

Inside, in the cool, a man
lies asleep on a pew, near
the tablet to seventeenth-century
Thomas Price, who "takes his nap
in our common mother's lap",
his dust a compatible neighbour
for the bronzed and breathing sleeper.

"Better death than long languishing",
says Cadogan's motto. Amen to that
on this day of heat and sleep,
amen! But after no long sickness
three small girls of one house came home
early from play. From their black memorial
one-year-old Mary cries "I was but young",
and claims eternal rest, being too tired
too soon.

The sleeping man wakes up. Outside,
the sunbathers have gone. A breeze mutes heat,
scampers over the graves, and starts
a susurration of grass, not unlike
whispers or stifled laughter.

'Cwmioie' is no. 5 in the sequence 'Singing to Wolves'

97

Thomas Price's
tablet in
Cwmioie (Cwmyoy)
church

Edgar Holloway,
Mountain Path,
1943
(Monnow
Valley Arts)

The Hedge

Ruth
Bidgood

Down the side of that sloping field
were old hawthorn trees, tall, wild,
all that was left of a hedge, no use any more
to divide or shelter, with those gaps
between trees, those branchy arches, waist-high,
shoulder-high, framing field or stream.

Now, back end of the year, farmer and boy
have cut the hawthorn, chain-saw groaning for hours,
great swathes of brushwood fringing a corridor
in which a few branches, spared, are being bent
into a new pleached hedge; stakes driven in,
wire strained, to make a flanking fence.

It will be a good hedge, woven to trim
density, bare slim boughs budding
here and there, pale yellow green, next spring;
the year after, trying a tentative
blossom again. Before too long
there should be shade and windbreak.

One day, far on, someone may stand
where I am now, across the river,
and say ' That's the old hedge, all run to ruin –
but look at the way those branches frame
parcels and plocks of beauty! Look now –
next winter is the cutting-time.'

99

Brian Hatton,
George 'Nurdy'
Saunders,
roadman
at Warham,
c.1908
(Hereford
Art Gallery)

In old deeds, small units of land are sometimes called 'parcels' or 'plocks'

Edward Kelly,
*A panel
with a
kneeling angel
from the
St Dubricius
polyptych in
Madley Church*

Resurrection Angels

Kilvert was told that people used to come to the Wild Duck Pool
on Easter morning "to see the sun dance and play in the water
and the angels who were at the Resurrection playing backwards
and forwards before the sun".

These were not troubling the waters
to bring healing. They were serving
no purpose. After the watch at the tomb,
the giving of good news, they were at play.
To and fro went the wings, to and fro
over the water, playing before the sun.

Stolid-seeming villagers stared
enchanted, watching sun dance and play,
light-slivers splinter water's dark.
In dazzle they half-saw
great shining shapes swoop frolicking
to and fro, to and fro.

                              This much was shared,
expected; day and place had their
appropriateness, their certainties.
The people had no words to tell
the astonishment, the individual bounty –
for each his own dance in the veins,
brush of wings on the soul.

Merthyr Clydawg

*Ruth
Bidgood*

Clodock; it sounds rustic, and English.
Clydawg; the lost Welsh is back. He seems
an off-beat martyr, killed for love,
out hunting, by a jealous rival; yet
a prince who led in battle and prayer,
his story has a spice of miracle. Oxen
(helped by a broken yoke) refused
to drag his body over the ford, insisted
that here should be his burial-place.

In the church, the gallery's music-table
might be straight from Hardy. But Latin
on a dug-up stone remembers
"that faithful woman the dear wife
Of Guinnda", who centuries back
lived in this place of shifting boundaries,
strife, loss, perpetual haunting, garbled names,
Welshness in the soil's depth,
unacknowledged riches,
uncomprehended power.

'Merthyr Clydawg' is no. 3 in the sequence 'Singing to Wolves'

101

Olchon Valley

*The Olchon Valley under the Black Mountains was in the
seventeenth century the refuge of an early Nonconformist
congregation, which had a number of offshoots.*

June has lit such a summer fire,
such a fire in the hedges! Sober hazel-leaves
tipped orange-pink, flare out of green,
burn translucent in the sun.

Once there was lit such a towering fire,
such a fire in the valley! Those who sat,
sober hearers, by hidden hearths, flared
out of homespun and leather, out of curbed flesh,
to spirit, to power, climbing, spreading –
flame the Word lit, words fanned.

Not a flame from that conflagration
breaks out here today, not a drift of its ashes
blurs the black slopes over the valley. But a fire
that was always here at the heart of quiet
gathers us into its congregation.

Patricio 2001 (part 1 of 'Guerinou')

*Patricio, with its holy well below the church, and old house of
Tŷ'n-y-Llwyn nearby, lies on the western side of Grwyne Fawr.
The ambush of the Norman lord Richard de Clare took place
on the eastern side.*

They have been bringing offerings
to the dark well, tying
rags to twigs in supplication, leaving
flowers to wilt in that chipped glass
uneasily perched on a dank ledge,
making crosses from bits of stick.

There seem so many of them, despite
the hiddenness of the place; as if
in a time of fear and shattering
these humble shapes are once more
valid – raw letters spelling out
helplessness, not yet
reshuffled into words of power.

103

Edgar Holloway,
*Capel-y-ffin:
towards Hay Bluff*,
1980
(Monnow
Valley Arts)

Singing to Wolves, Llanthony

"Why should we stay here
singing to wolves?" said Llanthony monks;
and left for soft living at the daughter-house,
finding themselves unloved by the Welsh,
and jaded with beautiful desolation –
just what the first anchorites had loved,
such wildness a treasure, not to be spoiled
by intrusive felling and tilling. All
they wanted was to contemplate heaven,
and the hills (almost as high), with herds of deer
ranging their tops.
                          The tidied ruins
are a favourite summer place. On this
burning day only children have spirit
to dash under arches, burst from shade to sun,
shifting points of colour, as intense
as flowers in baskets hung in front
of the crowded restaurant.

                              One tiny girl,
dark-haired, cool in a blue dress,
stays apart; alone she kneels on grass,
in the shade of the chapter-house wall,
carefully picking daisies. Perhaps she,
who knows? in her generation will be one
whose love is given to the remote, solitary,
trackless; to risk-encircled beauty;
deer on the marches of heaven; the sweet
unprofitable singing to wolves.

Tim Rossiter,
Llanthony Abbey

BRYAN ASPDEN

Nant Honddu
(for David Jones)

A grail of gorse; basketwork hedges
Threaded with birds. It's the end of March;
Spring still an outline map. These windflowers
And a purse of woodsorrel all that's filled in –

Two memories merging from the same month
Ten years apart, and at different ends of the path
That crosses your land and marks an eastern border.
When you were here you painted two black ponies

Grazing in a cup of the hills; a wattle fence;
Lopped ash and oak; a coverlet of fields;
Forestry rising to the shaved head of the moor –
A land man had neighboured long enough

To turn its grudge to giving – though the gifts
Weren't even-handed, nor was the taking.
You hankered for its comfort, grown up away.
After the first war came here to paint, to study, to recover.

David Jones, *Y Twmpa,*
Nant Honddu, 1926 (private collection)

You painted the river coming from Penny Beacon
Or Hay Bluff, past Capel-y-ffin, Pont-y-Wyrlod
To Garn Farm, Dôl Alice, Crucorney
Where three centuries of change have got their tongues
Round the place names, and Englished but not misplaced them.

Ten years ago I drove the Austin Cambridge
By the side of Nant Honddu, parked where the sign
Pointed a peglegged walker over Hatterall Hill
Away from Wales, to Hereford cattle and apples.

Today in the wind's gap above Bodfari I watch
Sheep, a sheepdog, two ponies; try to learn
Like you 'the creatureliness of things'; find
Some kindly forms, words that would heal the hurt
Of this land with its boundary in its heart.

David Jones, *Tir y Blaenau*, 1924-5
(Llyfrgell Gendlaethol Cymru/
The National Library of Wales)

Anne Stevenson

Orcop

(remembering Frances Horovitz, 1938-1983)

Driving south from Hereford one day in March
memorable for trickling piles of snow, with sideshows,
drift upon drift of snowdrops lapping the hedgerows,
we sighted the signpost and, on impulse, turned up
the winding, vertical road to Orcop. The church,
further away from the village than I remembered,
was no less an image of you than I remembered,
with its high-pitched, peasant roof and wooden steeple
gracing a slope with yew trees and a painter's view –
ploughed red soil, a pasture, a working barn –
that set it apart from the ordinary, just as your field stone,
when we found it, set you apart from the good people
labelled in polished marble, buried around you.
As in your life, though never aloof, you were alone.

I remembered how, when you quietly entered a room
in one of those woven dresses you used to wear,
heather or lavender, all senseless chattering would cease,
shamed by your dignity. I remembered your beautiful things:
your pots, your books, your cat, silver as your cross,
your delicate drawings. Yes, I remembered you exactly.
And there you were, still – beautiful, exceptional,
in a landscape of lichen I had to read like Braille
to find your name. I heard the first blackbird, then a thrush.
Later, as we left, the children we'd seen playing
Among the graves when we arrived resumed their game,
using your stone, a hump from another century,
to hide behind, while one, the smallest, counted slowly.

Walking Early by the Wye

Through dawn in February's wincing radiance,
every splinter of river mist
rayed in my eyes.

As if the squint of the sun had released light's
metals. As if the river pulsed white,
and the holly's

sharp green lacquered leaves leaped acetylene.
As if the air smouldered from the ice of dry
pain, as if day

were fragmented in doubt. As if it were given
to enter alive the braided rings Saturn
is known by

and yet be allied to the dyke's heaped mud.
I will not forget how the ash-trees stood,
silvered and still,

how each soft stone on its near shadow knelt,
how the sheep became stones where they built
Their pearled hill.

109

Sidney Richard
Percy,
The Wye,
1877
(private
collection)

The Parson and the Romany

A Black Mountain ballad to a Green Mountain tune (1982)

A parson went out one stormy day
To visit the sick in his valley grey.
A Romany girl he met on his way
With eyes like the radiant dawn of the day,
And she lived in the weather all around, all around,
She lived in the weather all around.

'Oh tell me, parson my love,' she said,
'Where are you going with your sickle head,
Your long black coat from your shoulder spread,
And your stoop like a monument to the dead,
When you live with the weather all around, all around,
When you live with the weather all around?'

'When you are as old as I, my lass,
You'll learn how the hard years press and pass,
For grief is the text and pain is the task,
And everyone belongs to the weeping class
While we live with the weather all around, all around,
While we live with the weather all around.'

'And what will you do when your time is done,
And you count up your sufferings one by one,
And put them in a sack with the string undone
For inspection by the Lord and his Ghost and Son
As we pray in the weather all around, all around,
As we pray in the weather all around?'

'Are you a demon or a sprite,' he cried,
'Do you speak out of ignorance or of pride?
Look up where the clouds are gaping wide
To show you the pillars of Hell inside,
While you laugh in the weather all around, all around,
While you laugh in the weather all around.'

'That's odd,' said the girl, 'for I've just come
From an angel who was sitting by a pillar of the sun.
He blessed me and called me his chosen one
And soon I'll be having a pretty little son
Who will live in the weather all around, all around,
Who will live in the weather all around.'

The parson, he shook off his cloak and his hood,
He threw back his head and laughed where he stood,
'Now tell me your name, O my wicked and good,'
'They call me the Lady of Kilpeck wood.'
So they danced in the weather of the sun, of the sun,
They danced in the weather of the sun.
They danced in the weather of the sun all around,
They danced in the weather of the sun.

111

Joshua Cristall,
*A Peasant Girl
Shading Her Eyes*,
1812
(Yale Center
for British Art)

112

Brian Hatton,
The Farm,
Warham,
1910
(Hereford
Art Gallery)

ANNE CLUYSENAAR

October 1

For Esther de Waal and Hilary Llewellyn-Williams

She's up that old plum-tree, bare-footed,
pitchfork in hand. And now the grass,
warmed by October sun, receives them,
blue-white with bloom, cool to bite.

Her son made her promise not to climb.
But, 'As you're here,' she asks, looking down,
'surely it must be all right?' Her smile
reminds of a hunting cat up a tree.

'Old men should be explorers.' Old women
have to be, surely. With change and death
crossing the very threshold. Beyond,
the sun, the leaves, the fruit. As ever.

Winter on the way. I'll have jam from these.
But I think too of a younger friend
starting her marriage, enjoying right now
our housewarming gifts, their delicate bloom.

January 1

The drive is free of snow and our neighbour
has brought us two big round bales of hay
which together we bounce off his tail-board. The pinch
he lifts to my nose holds the smell of summer.

And the girl who was taught by someone forgotten
how to know good hay, stands here forgetting
seventy years of her own life, sniffing
so many herbs, nothing coarse, no must.

What does it matter who stands here? That smell
will be just as good in a thousand years.
Though so much else will be changed, I hope
that girl or that woman loves it as I do

and stands in a barn, by a rick, down a tunnel,
wherever. When snow has fallen, she can reach
as I do for armfuls of meadow-hay, rich
with sun and the touch of bees and butterflies.

113

114

Joshua Cristall,
*Interior of
a Stable*,
1829
(Tate Gallery)

BONNIE THURSTON

St Mary's Church, Craswall

We didn't intend to come here,
were on our way to Hay,
to bank, books, lunch.
But her presence there,
Queen of the Monnow Valley,
required attendance.

She is an unprepossessing church,
low, square, sturdy,
weather-boarded bell turret
(perhaps without a bell?),
old fives court, a cockpit on the north,
the west end walled for a school.
Stone seating on the south faces
the base for a preaching cross
where only rotten wood remains.

The porch door was locked,
but the nave door –
a thing of old, solid planks,
iron bands, heavy, circular handle –
groaned into carefully tended space.
Lit by perpendicular east windows
from a priory Edward IV dissolved.

In dull morning light
the few bits of brass gleamed;
the pots of local flowers were fresh;
the life of something ancient
that guidebooks never mention
was alive and well and palpable.

One never knows when errands
on ordinary, overcast days
will swing open into places of love.

115

Edgar Holloway,
Craswall II, 1991
(Monnow Valley Arts)

Charles F. Walker:
Top, *Wacton*;
Middle, *Staunton
on Wye*;
Bottom,
Bishops Frome
Far right, *Kilpeck*;
(Herefordshire
Libraries)

Sheela-na-gig on Kilpeck Church

Squatting under the eaves,
lewdly grinning down at us,
exposing yourself to all comers,
who brought you to church?
What raucous imagination
dared make you
an ecclesiastical decoration?

One which loved fleshly life,
knew sex is hilarious
and procreation normal;
one which explored
a woman's body and found
treasures in darkness
and riches in secret places.

Norman Churches, Herefordshire

Escaping turbulent Oxford
I used to bike to Iffley,
sit in the shadows
of that Norman church
and breathe easier.
I did not know
what drew me,
only that it soothed,
calmed, centered.

Thirty years later
I glimpse the why
here, in these churches
built of local stone,
churches that seem
to rise from earth
as naturally as hedgerows
and as full of life.

Their square simplicity
is softened
by arch and apse.
No ornate fan vaulting
draws the eye upward.
Homey dog-toothed arches
tie walls firmly to floor,
make the place solid,
embracing, permanent.

Unpretentious churches
house a practical
life of spirit.
No lace cuffs ever offered
or incense accompanied
the coarse broken bread,
the pewter cup
of rough wine
that tastes of earth.

Unpretentious churches
root the life of this land
in the practice of prayer,
at many crossroads
quietly offer all comers
an invitation to pause,
to rest, to remember
that peace passes
understanding.

Jim Dening

Herefordshire Ways of Looking at a Barn (Ledbury 2014)

For twenty years we've come past here
(the walkers say), while leaning on their sticks,
and two old dogs are anxious to agree;
it's been a landmark for us of a sort
beneath its rust-red corrugated roof,
subsiding broken-jointed into earth.

Two hundred years, who knows, and more,
this place has stood rough-built beside the track
(the orchard grower says), the old carts
went up for charcoal and coppiced staves,
deepening the holloway between the trees,
while overhead the buzzard hangs and mews.

First thing here was get the levels right
(the builder says), we had the digger in,
a kango on the rock beneath the floor;
we must have had two hundred ton away
until we squared him up, jacked the frame,
cut out the rot and spliced new oak in.

Wormholes (the sand blaster says) go barely
half an inch, old oak inside still breaks the drill.
We made new ironwork (the blacksmith says),
catches and handles all beaten and swaged.
Tiling's finished (the roofer says), I'll fix
the downpipe at the gulley and flaunch him in.

Where has the old barn gone? (say the owl and the swallow,
the bat, the badger, the weasel, the fox and the rabbit),
where are our burrows and perches, where are the ivy
and old smells and dark corners? Where is our home?

119

Brian Hatton,
*Landscape
with shed
and hayrick*,
1901-16
(Hereford
Art Gallery)

In the Borderlands

Beside old roads you see them,
the ditch and bank of other times,
the deer park of an ancient hundred,
the tribal boundary,
a claim of sovereignty
intended to contain and to exclude;
the struggling sweating men long dead,
their sharp defences overgrown,
their falling earthworks fading in the mist,
the echoes of their voices all but gone.
–   I had another sheepdog once, see?
came a voice along the bar:
he ran off on Offa's Dyke one day,
in a place where rustling aspen grow
so thick you're not sure where you are.
I heard him in the bushes growl and bark,
the wind was blowing strong and sharp
and turning over every silver leaf;

up flew the birds, all you saw of them
was rooks far-flung around the sky.
I heard the bark turn into a whimper
and my old dog came limping back
his leg all bloody and fur a-clotted,
I could tell from looking in his eye
he'd seen a thing invisible to me;
with the wind increasing all the time
I seemed to hear men's voices shouting
and footsteps running and the clash of iron;
with the aspen lashing all the time,
a whirring in the air, a flying branch
or something heavy whacked me to the ground,
my shoulder took a vicious twinge;
I thought it high time to be out of there
and back here for a pint and living company.
My old dog was always quiet after that,
he'd look at me sidelong and anxious-like.

OFFA'S DYKE - BRADNOR HILL

Edgar Holloway 1985

121

Edgar
Holloway,
*Offa's Dyke,
Bradnor Hill,*
1985
(Monnow
Valley Arts)

Margot Miller

Hole in the Wall

That day she seemed drawn, pulled towards the river
She had to, must bathe in the dark green water
I looked upstream, sensing the great Welsh flow

She climbed carefully from the rock, sank in the deeper pool
Set off, swam out to the middle where the current pulls
I felt Great Grandma Gwy tugging, pushing her

Come to me, *Dewchei mi*, Dusty *tirion*
I'll take you down, down where I curve and bend
beneath the hills I've carved, further down to the Forest

The rain began to fall, showering droplets, ringing the water
'Swim the other way,' I called, 'Go upstream, 'gainst the flow!'
I thought, 'Don't take her down, past Holy Well and Foy

Not downstream in your powerful arms.' Dusty turned,
Laughing, puffing, swam against the river's strength
'Don't go too far up – come back now,' I called again

Her brown hair bobbed between the rain and river
She dived below – came up shaking her sparkly head
and gave a little shout of *joie de vivre*

From the solid rock, I prayed, pleaded
'Great Mistress of *Afon* – let her go – *Mam-gu*
Release her – carry her back to me
Quickly – safely – here – now'

122

Hole in the Wall is a hamlet beside the River Wye
Afon Gwy in the Welsh language is the name for the River Wye
Dusty is the poet's daughter

Above: Edward Kelly, *Fish, Ross on Wye* (stone platter)
Opposite: Edward Kelly, *Moonlight – River Wye, Hoarwithy*
The artist writes:
The painting is structured on a grid.
The water flows in a myriad of directions and forms and colours.
Diagonal thrust – a large bird takes flight top left – flapping wings.
A small form shelters silently bottom right.
Two swans meet – an assignation – indeed a heart shape at centre.
Fish gently bob – plant forms reflect in water.
A mostly silent intimate world under the moonlight.
The river remains the only truly natural environment
in the midst of intensive farming.

Martin Griffiths,
Sunset, Bromyard to Hereford Road

The lives of the poets: a chronology

WILLIAM DE WYCOMBE (fl. *c*.1275), a Benedictine from Reading Abbey, composed polyphonic anthems and songs. While Precentor of the Priory at Leominster, a cell of Reading Abbey, he had to copy for his choir musical and other manuscripts, a burden which, 'though it may have appeared small,' he wrote, was considerable. He wrote dozens of bright 'alleluyas', all but one now known only from fragments or from mention in an index. He copied the round (or 'rota') 'Sumer is icomen in', and probably had composed it. Musicians admire William's use of six-part polyphony; his text is amongst the first lyrics in English.

SIR JOHN CLANVOWE (*c*.1341-1391) of Hergest and Yazor was a knight in Brittany, Poitou and Picardy. He joined John of Gaunt's *chevauchée* (1373-4) from Calais to Bordeaux and in 1378 shared command in Gaunt's army. Clanvowe was favoured by Humphrey Bohun, Earl of Hereford, and by Kings Edward III and Richard II, becoming a knight of the King's Chamber. Among his friends was Geoffrey Chaucer. He wrote both *The Boke of Cupide* and *The Two Ways*, a book of lay piety. Between 1381 and 1385 he undertook commissions in Wales and the Marches. As ambassador he treated for England's peace with France and, in Portugal, concerning John of Gaunt's claims in Castile. Clanvowe and Sir William Neville, his comrade in arms and fellow Chamber Knight, were suspected of Lollardy in 1390. They left London and joined Louis de Bourbon's crusade against piratical Moors on the Barbary Coast. The following year Clanvowe and Neville travelled to Constantinople where Clanvowe died, 'causing his companion on the march, Sir William Neville . . . such inconsolable sorrow that he never took food again and two days afterward breathed his last, greatly mourned, in the same village' (*Westminster Chronicle*, 1391). Above their grave in the church of Galata beside the Golden Horn a tombstone showed the family arms of each impaled with the arms of the other as for a married couple, their helms nearly touching.

MICHAEL DRAYTON (1563-1631) was born in Warwickshire. In London he enjoyed the company of Ben Jonson and of the antiquaries John Stowe and William Camden. He wrote odes, eclogues (*The Shepheards Garland*), satires and historical poems. Among his sonnets is the much admired 'Since there's no help, come let us kiss and part . . .' Drayton was buried in Westminster Abbey; Lady Anne Clifford paid for his monument.

JOHN DAVIES OF HEREFORD (1565-1618) as a calligrapher was considered by Thomas Fuller to be 'the greatest master of the pen that England in her age beheld'. Pepys was pleased to own a sample of his writing. By 1605 Davies' writing-pupils in London included Prince Henry and many of the eminent. Davies moved in the circle of Donne, Jonson and Fletcher. His output of sonnets, satires, epigrams and celebratory verse was considerable. Volumes included *Microcosmos* (1603), *The Scourge of Folly* (?1611), *The Muse's Sacrifice* (1612) and *Wits Bedlam* (1617). Mary Croft of Croft Castle was his first wife; together they are buried in St Dunstan-in-the-West, London.

HENRY VAUGHAN THE SILURIST (1621-95) was born in Llansantffraed on the Usk, a twin brother to Thomas. 'English is a language the Author was not born to.' Schooled first under Matthew Herbert, Rector of Llangattock, 'the pride of our Latinity,' the brothers went on to Jesus College, Oxford. Thomas stayed there 'ten or 12 years'; Henry moved to the Inns of Court to study law 'which the sudden eruption of our late civil warres wholie frustrated'. He took up arms for the Royalist cause at Rowton Heath, near Chester (1645), then retired to Llansantffraed. By the Usk, despite the puritan ascendancy, he was able to cherish the spirituality of the English Church. He published poems and prose religious works, studied hermetical texts, made botanical notes, and practised as a country doctor. Vaughan was married first to Catherine Wise, who bore him four children, then to her sister Elizabeth, who bore another four.

THOMAS TRAHERNE (1637-74), 'a shoemaker's son of Hereford', went to Brasenose College, Oxford (BA 1656). Rector of Credenhill, he served as bishop's surrogate in the Consistory Court. Credenhill's churchwardens tell that Traherne was 'a good and godly man, well learned' who 'visited the poor and instructed the youth'. In 1669 he became chaplain to Sir Orlando Bridgeman, Lord Keeper of the Seal, but till 1673 the churchwardens report: 'Our minister is continually resident

among us.' He died soon after moving to Bridgeman's home in Teddington. Edward Harley lamented: 'My worthy friend, Thomas Traherne . . . dead.' Traherne's handwritten *Poems and Centuries of Meditations*, found in 1896, were published in 1903 and 1906. He was a visionary who delighted in love and felicity: 'Never was anything in this world loved too much.' The image, which illustrates the phrase 'You are as prone to love as the sun is to shine', is from one of four windows dedicated to Traherne made by Tom Denny and installed in Hereford Cathedral.

JOHN PHILIPS (1676-1709), son and grandson of parsons in the Hereford Diocese, learned to cultivate apples at Withington Court, the family's home, and at Eau Withington, the home of William Brome. Schooled at Winchester, Philips attended Christ Church, Oxford. His poem *The Splendid Shilling* (1705) was followed by *Blenheim*, a satiric twist on that battle written at the behest of Edward Harley and Lord Bolingbroke. *Cyder* (1708), modelled on Virgil's *Georgics*, purports to instruct those who tend orchards. Philips liked to smoke a pipe of tobacco, 'companion fit of Pleasantry, and Wine'; he was to die in Hereford aged 33 of consumption. A monument to Philips is in the north transept of Hereford Cathedral, another in Westminster Abbey. James Thomson in *The Seasons* (1730) praised 'Philips, Pomona's bard' for his 'rhyme-unfettered verse'.

WILLIAM DIAPER (1685-1717) from Bridgwater, Somerset, was 'bred in a homely Cott'. He attended Balliol College, Oxford, and served as curate of Brent. In the poem *Brent* he bemoaned its floods. *Nereides* and *Sea Eclogues* applied pastoral tradition to the aqueous world of mermen and mermaids. In *Dryades* (1712) Diaper introduces fairies, nymphs and dryads into well-observed English countryside. Like John Philips he found occasion to praise Bolingbroke and Oxford (Edward Harley). He eulogises Philips, 'who once Silurian Plains adorn'd,' whose mantle as a georgic poet Diaper seemed set to inherit. Jonathan Swift considered the poem *Dryades* 'a very good one' and secured for Diaper an allowance and a living, for he was 'in a nasty Garret, very sick'. Diaper translated some Horace. He died aged 31.

ALEXANDER POPE (1688-1744) was largely self-educated. His *Pastorals*, written when he was sixteen, were noticed by Jacob Tonson, the publisher, who included them in his influential *Miscellany*. The *Rape of the Lock* and verse translations of the *Iliad* and the *Odyssey* established Pope's eminence. In Twickenham he gardened, built a grotto, and developed the aesthetic of the picturesque. The *Dunciad* (1729) ridiculed contemporaries. Moral and intellectual poems characterised his last decade – *An Essay on Man*; *Moral Essays*; and several *Epistles*, including that to Dr Arbuthnot. Pope learned about Herefordshire while a guest at Holme Lacy to the Scudamores and at Ledbury to Jacob Tonson, who had retired to The Hazel.

JOHN DYER (1699-1757), born in Carmarthenshire, went to school at Westminster. Successively he was apprentice-lawyer in Wales, artist in London, traveller in Italy, farm-manager in Bromyard, and Rector in Leicestershire and in Lincolnshire. *Grongar Hill* (1726) is inspired by his homeland in the Vale of the Towey; *The Ruins of Rome* (1740) draws on Italian observations; *The Fleece* (1757), a long georgic, celebrates wise shepherding. Dyer gives prominence in *The Fleece* to Herefordshire, its sheep, shepherds and pastures. His poem also describes the techniques of spinning, weaving, dyeing and trade in wool.

WILLIAM BOYCE (1711-1799), once a choirboy at St Paul's, composed anthems, eight symphonies, twelve overtures, and the masque *Peleus and Thetis*. From 1737 for eighteen years, it seems, he directed the orchestra at the annual two-day Three Choir's Festival of Hereford, Gloucester and Worcester. For it he wrote a *Worcester Overture*. Boyce composed *Hearts of Oak*, a favourite of the navy. *The Herefordshire Winter*, printed in 1730 on a single sheet folio, was his first published work. Later the song appeared in *The Agreeable Amusement* (1743-4). Boyce was appointed Master of the King's Musick (1755) and organist at the Chapel Royal (1758). He edited *Cathedral Music*. His body is buried beneath the centre of St Paul's dome.

RICHARD PAYNE KNIGHT (1751-1824) designed Downton Castle and its park beside the River Teme. His ideal of the picturesque was shaped by Johann Winckelmann and Jacob van Ruisdael, Pope's poetry, Gilpin's travel-notes, and discussions with Uvedale Price. *The Landscape: a didactic poem* (1794) influenced design and taste. *The Progress of Civil Society* (1796) argued for political and moral freedom. Knight startled classicists by arguing that Homer was not the author of *The Odyssey*, that the Elgin Marbles were mere Roman copies, and that phallic symbolism underlay much religious art. A Whig, Knight sat as MP for Leominster in 1780, then Ludlow from 1784 to 1806.

ROBERT BLOOMFIELD (1766-1823) worked as a boy on a farm in Suffolk. Insufficiently robust for that tough life, he went to London where he was apprenticed as a cobbler, made Aeolian harps and wrote poems. *The Farmer's Boy* (1800) – 1,500 lines of heroic couplets – won Southey's and Wordsworth's admiration, and gave him some relief from poverty. In 1807, on the invitation of Thomas Baker of Stroud, Bloomfield boated down the Wye. Reduced to penury through the fraud of a publisher, he moved his family from expensive London to Bedfordshire.

WILLIAM WORDSWORTH (1770-1850), born in Cockermouth, attended St John's, Cambridge, and lived for two years in the Quantock Hills where Samuel Taylor Coleridge and he jointly produced *Lyrical Ballads* (1798). William, Dorothy (his sister) and Mary Hutchinson (whom William married) settled near Grasmere in the Lake District. In 1793 and 1798 Wordsworth walked beside the Wye. William came to know Herefordshire when he, Mary and Dorothy visited Mary's brother, Tom Hutchinson, who farmed near Kington and later at Brinsop Court. The Wordsworths first stayed at Brinsop in 1827. William Wordsworth became Poet Laureate in 1843.

ELIZABETH BARRETT BROWNING (1806-61), educated in her father's library at Hope End in Colwall, exchanged letters with literary neighbours including Uvedale Price. *The Battle of Marathon*, a long poem, was published when she was 14. EBB loved the Malvern Hills, but when she was 26 her father's sugar revenues collapsed, so he moved his family to Sidmouth and then London. In Wimpole Street EBB, held to be in frail health, lived, read and wrote largely in a curtained bedroom, but corresponded with an admirer of her poems, Robert Browning. Married secretly in 1846, they left for Italy where, held in mutual love, EBB thrived. Casa Guidi in Florence became the Brownings' home. EBB's *Sonnets from the Portuguese* appeared in 1850, *Aurora Leigh* in 1857, *Last Poems* in 1862.

FRANCIS KILVERT (1840-79), diarist, studied at Wadham College, Oxford. He was assistant-curate to his father in Wiltshire and, from 1865 to 1872, to Revd Richard Lister Venables in Clyro. Kilvert returned to Bredwardine as rector for what proved to be the last two years of his life. He married Elizabeth Rowland from Oxfordshire on 20 August 1879. Thirty-three days later he died and is buried at Bredwardine. His diaries describe long walks from Clyro amid the hills, encounters with the poor, with the aged, with joyful children and with lovely young women. Kilvert's entries, compassionate and observant, record joyfully the loveliness of people and their country ways in the neighbourhood of Hay.

EDMUND GEORGE VALPY KNOX (EVOE) (1870-1970), poet and satirist, chose the pseudonym Evoe. From 1932 to 1949 he edited *Punch*. His brothers, sons of a staunch evangelical bishop of Manchester, were likewise remarkable: Ronald Knox, a witty Monsignor and Bible translator; 'Dilly' Knox, codebreaker; and Wilfred Knox, low-church priest and scholar. Penelope Fitzgerald, Evoe's daughter, wrote of their diverse lives in *The Knox Brothers*. Evoe, for *Punch*, was noted for quick satires in the style of great poets. He managed hilariously to evoke a poet's manner without resorting to a parody of any particular poem.

JOHN MASEFIELD (1879-1967), Ledbury-born, went to Warwick School, then in 1891, having been orphaned, to the training-ship *HMS Conway*. In 1894 he sailed for Chile round the Horn, then to New York, where he jumped ship. Masefield retained enthusiasm for tall-ships, and for the traditions, language and shanties of those who sailed in them. *Salt-water Ballads* was published in 1902. The ruffian society of Ledbury was the scene of his long poem *The Everlasting Mercy*. *Reynard the Fox* celebrated rural life and its pathos. In 1930 Masefield became Poet Laureate.

SIEGFRIED SASSOON (1886-1967) was educated at Marlborough and at Clare College, Cambridge. *Memoirs of a Fox-Hunting Man* (1928) tells of his life in Kent and Sussex before the First World War. A Second Lieutenant in the trenches, Sassoon wrote wry verse, tender towards those in his command, critical of war leaders and patriotic cant. Awarded the MC for bravery, he cast it away. As he edged towards disloyalty, he was diagnosed as 'shell-shocked' and dispatched to Craiglockhart Hospital in Edinburgh, where he encouraged fellow patient Wilfred Owen. Sassoon's war poems were published in *The Old Huntsman* (1917) and *Counter-Attack* (1918). Later poems showed love for the countryside and a spirituality inspired by George Herbert and Henry Vaughan.

ROLAND MATHIAS (1915-1996) was born near Talybont-on-Usk. His father, an army chaplain, moved his family to the Rhineland, Salisbury Plain and Aldershot. Roland attended school in Surrey, then Jesus College, Oxford. He read history and gained a B. Litt., then taught in St Helens. During the war, as a conscientious objector, he was twice sentenced to three months hard labour. Early poems were published in *The Welsh Review* and *The Listener*. Headmaster of Pembroke Dock Grammar School (1948-1958), he began editing the *Anglo-Welsh Review*. Collections of his poems were published, and the historical work *Whitsun Riot* (1963). Later, he was headmaster of King Edward VI, School, Birmingham, and then, moving to Brecon, he promoted the literature of Wales.

RUTH BIDGOOD (b.1922) was schooled in Port Talbot, read English at Oxford, and during World War II served as a coder in Alexandria. In 1964 she and her husband bought a small house in Abergwesyn, Breconshire. It became Ruth's full time home in 1974. She found, she said, 'the call of the land and the ruins drawing me up the side-valleys into the remains of communities'. Her poems are conversational, gentle, consoling, in touch with violence in the past and the bleakness that some endure. Ruth writes warmly about the Vale of Ewyas and visits to Herefordshire. Alert with her pen into her nineties, Ruth now lives in Beulah.

BRYAN ASPDEN (1933-99). Bryan was born in Blackburn, Lancashire, studied English at Durham University, and lived from 1965 in Conway, north Wales. He was a local government officer in Llandudno, learnt Welsh, and wrote in that language too. Bryan was a Quaker. His poems are collected in *News of the Changes* (1984) and *Blind Man's Meal* (1988).

ANNE STEVENSON (b.1933). Anne was born in Cambridge, England, grew up in New England and Michigan, and studied music and literature in Ann Arbor. In 1964 she settled in Britain. Anne has published critical biographies of Elizabeth Bishop and Sylvia Plath. She has lived in Cambridge, Glasgow, Dundee, Oxford, where she was Fellow of Lady Margaret Hall, and in Hay on Wye, where with Michael Farley and Alan Halsey she established The Poetry Bookshop. Anne's poems reveal a rational, kind, humorous sensibility effervescing with ideas and wit.

FLEUR ADCOCK (b.1934) was born in New Zealand, and after some childhood years in England, returned to university in Wellington and became a lecturer, a librarian, and a friend to NZ poets. In 1973 she moved to London. Ten books of poems have been published, including her *Collected Poems 1960-2000*. Many of her poems explore identity, rootlessness, and the poignancy of the lives of some women. 'The tone I feel at home in is one in which I can address people without embarrassing them. I should like them to relax and listen as if to an intimate conversation.'

RONALD JOHNSON (1935-98), born in Ashland, Kansas, was drafted into the US army, then attended Columbia University. Jonathan Williams and he walked the Appalachian Trail. For two years they were foot-loose in England and Wales. *The Book of the Green Man* (1967) tells how they searched for all things 'most rich, most glittering, most strange' as they walked up the Wye Valley in the spring of 1963. Later, Johnson lived in San Francisco. His poems include *ARK* (1996), modernist and long, and *The Shrubberies*.

ANNE CLUYSENAAR (1936-2014) was born in Belgium. Her parents were painters, each part-Belgian, part-Scottish. Pre-war they moved to Britain and on to Connemara, Ireland. Anne learned Gaelic, studied Literature at Trinity College, Dublin (1953-7), and helped launch *Icarus*, in which her poems appeared. At universities she lectured on linguistics. Settling on a smallholding near Usk, Anne co-founded and edited *Scintilla* for the Vaughan Society. She wrote: 'Perhaps I have found myself so deeply and enduringly attracted by Vaughan's poetry, though I am not a Royalist and have no special attachment to Christian doctrine, because I recognise in him spiritual impulses which are central to all human life.'

FRANCES HOROVITZ (1938-83) graduated in English and Drama from Bristol and went to RADA in London (1959-61). In 1964 she married fellow-poet Michael Horovitz. Her sensitive poetry readings on radio were admired. Frances visited the Carmelite monastery at Aylesford – the *Aylesford Review* published her *Poems* in 1967. She and Michael bought a cottage in Slad, near Stroud where their son Adam was born. Her poems were published in *The High Tower* (1970), *Water over Stone* (1980) and *Snow Light, Water Light* (1983). With poet Roger Garfitt, Frances lived in Rowlestone, then in Northumberland from 1980, then again in Herefordshire – in St Weonards, above Orcop. Frances and Roger married just four weeks before her early death.

BONNIE THURSTON earned a BA in English at Bethany College in her home state of West Virginia. For her MA and PhD she studied literature and religion and the thought of Thomas Merton. She is the author or editor of nineteen theological books and five small collections of poetry, three published in Wales. She now lives quietly in the West Virginia hills where she gardens, cooks, reads, writes, and enjoys classical music. She visits the UK frequently and knows Herefordshire through her friendship with Esther de Waal.

JIM DENING attended St Edmund Hall, Oxford. A business journalist, then book publisher, he founded Archive Editions, which preserves documents on political and diplomatic history and now is part of Cambridge University Press. He initiated the International Boundaries Research Unit in the University of Durham. Jim has lived in France, writes poetry in French as in English, and performs with a satirical/absurdist band in Ledbury, where he now lives. His poems are collected in *pebbles, debris* (2003) and *Dealing with the edge* (2011).

MARGOT MILLER spent her young days in Surrey. After marriage, she studied sociology at Kingston-on-Thames University. She has an MA too in English literature. Margot has lived in the Cotswolds, Oxford and Glastonbury. In 2001 she settled in Fownhope. With Sue Sharp, Margot edited in 2010 an anthology, *Landscapes on the Edge – Poems of the Wye Valley and Welsh Borders*. She is author of an Iron Age historical novel, *The Priestess of Endor – a Celtic Journey* (2002) and of *Ogham – The Magical Celtic Tree Alphabet* (2012). Margot helped to found the Mortimer History Society. She is researching the life of St Dubricius (or Dyfrig), sixth-century evangelist of Ergyng and of south-east Wales.

The poems: sources

Adcock, Fleur, *Poems 1960-2000* (Bloodaxe Books, 2000)

Aspden, Bryan, *News of Changes* (Seren, 1984)

Bidgood, Ruth, *New and Selected Poems* (Seren, 2004); *Singing to Wolves* (Seren, 2000); *Symbols of Plenty* (Seren, 2006); *Time Being* (Seren, 2009)

Bloomfield, Robert, *The Banks of Wye* (London, 1811)

Boyce, William (composer); words anon. Text supplied by Michael Tavinor, Dean of Hereford.

Browning, Elizabeth Barrett, *Poetical Works in Six Volumes* (Smith, Elder & Co., 1890)

Clanvowe, John, *The Boke of Cupide, God of Love*, ed. V.J. Scattergood (D.S. Brewer Ltd, 1965)

Cluysenaar, Anne, *Touching Distances: diary poems* (Cinnamon Press, 2014)

Davies, John of Hereford, introductory verses to Rowland Vaughan's *Most Approved and Long Experienced Water-Works*, (George Eld, 1610)

Dening, Jim, Ms from the poet. See also *pebbles, debris* (Arcade, 2003)

Diaper, William, *The Complete Works*, ed. Dorothy Broughton (Routledge & Kegan Paul, 1952)

Drayton, Michael, *The Complete Works* (John Russell-Smith, 1876)

Dyer, John, *Poems* (J. Dodsley, in Pall-mall, 1770)

Horovitz, Frances, *Rowlestone Haiku*, with Roger Garfitt (Five Seaons Press)*; The Kilpeck Anthology*, ed. Glenn Storhaug (Five Seasons Press, 1981); *Collected Poems* (Bloodaxe, 1984)

Johnson, Ronald, *The Book of the Green Man* (Longmans, Green & Co., 1967)

Kilvert, Francis, *The Hereford Times* on dates shown

Knight, Richard Payne, *The Landscape*, (London, 1795)

Knox, E.V. ('Evoe'), *Punch* magazine (1921)

Masefield, John, *Collected Poems* (Heinemann, 1932)

Mathias, Roland, *Collected Poems* (University of Wales, 2002)

Miller, Margot, from the anthology *Landscapes on the Edge: Poems of the Wye Valley*, edited by Margot Miller and Sue Sharp (Fineleaf, 2010)

Philips, John, *Cyder, a poem in two books* (Jacob Tonson, 1708)

Pope, Alexander, *The Works* (Wordsworth Editions, 1995)

Sassoon, Siegfried, *Collected Poems 1908-1956* (Faber and Faber 1961)

Stevenson, Anne, *Poems 1955-2005* (Bloodaxe, 2004); *Stone Milk* (Bloodaxe, 2007)

Thurston, Bonnie Bowman, *Belonging to Borders* (Liturgical Press, Collegeville, Minnesota); *A Place to Pay Attention* (Cinnamon 2014); *The Heart's Land* (Three Peaks Press, 2001)

Traherne, Thomas, *The Poetical Works*, ed. Bertram Dobell (Dobell, 1903); *Centuries* (Clarendon, 1960)

Vaughan, Henry, *Poetry and Selected Prose*, ed. L.C. Martin (OUP, 1963)

Wordsworth, William, *Poetical Works*, ed. Thomas Hutchinson (OUP, 1916)

The lives of the painters: a chronology

CHRISTOPHER SAXTON (*c.*1540-*c.*1610) produced the first county maps of England and Wales. Map making in the reign of Elizabeth I was made possible by advances in surveying technology and printing from engraved copper plates. Accurate mapping of the whole country became increasingly important. In 1574 Saxton began the survey of England. The first plates were engraved by 1574 and in 1578 the survey was complete. Individual county sheets were issued before the completed survey was issued as an atlas in 1579.

SIR GODFREY KNELLER (born Gottfried Kniller 1646-1723) was the leading portrait painter in England during the late 17th and early 18th centuries, and court painter to monarchs from Charles II to George I. His major works include 'The Chinese Convert'; a series of four portraits of Isaac Newton; a series of ten European monarchs, including King Louis XIV of France; over 40 portraits of members of the Kit-Cat Club; and ten 'beauties' of the court of William III.

THOMAS GAINSBOROUGH (1727-1788) was born in Suffolk, where he painted portraits of his daughters and of squires and their families. He became known among the fashionable in Bath from 1759. Amongst the first to commission a portrait was Uvedale Tomkyns Price of Herefordshire, owner of Foxley. Price's grandson, Uvedale Price recalled his own 'frequent excursions with [Gainsborough] into the country'. In 1769 Gainsborough became a founding member of the Royal Academy. His portraits, such as 'The Blue Boy' and 'Mrs Siddons', are esteemed as amongst Britain's highest artistic achievements.

ANTHONY DEVIS (1728-1816) was from Preston, Lancashire; the portraitist Arthur Devis was his half-brother. Anthony, attuned to the picturesque, travelled widely to sketch and paint English scenery, often at the behest of landowners. From his late teens his home was in London. In 1786 Devis retired to Albury House, near Guildford, where he collected curios and paintings.

NICHOLAS POCOCK (1740-1821), of a seafaring family, captained a Bristol merchant ship. He embellished his logbooks with pen-and-wash drawings of shipping and harbours in South Carolina, Dominica, Nevis, St Kitts, and the Mediterranean. At 38 he settled in Bristol, painting watercolours of ships, the sea, the city, and a journey to the Wye. He moved to Westminster in 1789. Admirals commissioned Pocock to depict their victories. He studied how waves and weather were during the course of a sea-battle, how the fleet had been positioned, and how ships appeared. Pocock was aboard *Pegasus* during Rodney's battle of the Glorious First of June. He contributed six etchings for *The Life of Admiral Lord Nelson*. Pocock was a founder of the Society of Painters in Watercolours.

THOMAS HEARNE (1744-1817) was for six years an apprentice engraver. In 1771 he travelled to the Leeward Islands commissioned by the new Governor, Sir Ralph Payne, to paint twenty large landscapes. He returned in 1775 and travelled with Sir George Beaumont in England, Scotland and Wales to provide eighty-four drawings for *The Antiquities of Great Britain* (1778-1781). At Downton for Richard Payne Knight he drew and painted, and he illustrated Knight's poem *The Landscape*. Hearne typically chose to use a tinted wash or subdued watercolour over a precise outline in pencil or pen. Dr Thomas Monro collected Hearne's works and showed them in Adelphi Terrace, London, as models for younger artists to copy.

JOSHUA CRISTALL (1768-1847). The Cristall family, makers of ship's tackle, were from Cornwall and moved to Rotherhithe. At the Royal Academy Schools Cristall studied engraving. Better, he entered a circle of watercolourists under Dr Thomas Monro's patronage. John and Cornelius Varley invited him in 1802 to sketch with them in Dolgellau. Meanwhile Joshua's sister, Ann, a poet, had become a friend of Mary Wollstonecraft. Cristall painted landscapes, scenes from literature, and figures in pastoral settings. He married (1812) Elizabeth Cossins who ran a school for young ladies in the Manor House on London's Paddington Green, which

became a resort for musicians, artists and authors. In 1822 Elizabeth and Joshua move to rural life in Goodrich near the Wye. There they lived for eighteen idyllic years in Granton Cottage, a simple house with studio and stable. Elizabeth and Joshua are buried in St Giles's churchyard.

JAMES WARD (1769-1859) was early influenced by his brother-in-law George Morland to paint genre scenes. From 1810, admiring Rubens, he painted horses prancing, fighting or startled. Gentry commissioned him to paint their horses, dogs, children, portraits and estates. His composition 'The Levett Children of Wynchnor, Staffordshire, the two youngest on a donkey', is gloriously happy. Ward's enormous landscape 'Gordale Scar' (1814), for Lord Ribblesdale, expresses the sublime in nature. Admired as 'The Mammoth of Animal Painters', Ward painted Marengo, Napoleon's spirited horse, and Copenhagen, the horse of the Duke of Wellington. In 1830 he moved from London to Cheshunt in Hertfordshire.

JOSEPH MALLORD WILLIAM TURNER (1775-1851), watercolorist and painter in oils, was hailed by John Ruskin as the artist who could most 'stirringly and truthfully measure the moods of nature ... the greatest of the age'. His paintings of shimmering climatic effects and of pure, evanescent light still win great admiration. He first visited Wales and the Marches in 1793. He established a routine of touring and sketching in summers and painting in a London studio in winters. Turner had a remarkable visual memory and was effortless in draughtsmanship. This portrait of him is by Cornelius Varley.

JOHN VARLEY (1778-1842), born in Hackney, exhibited in the Royal Academy from 1798. He is recognised as a father-figure of plein-air painting. From sketching tours of Wales in 1798/9 and 1802, and of Hereford, Leominster and Chester, he returned to London with accurate studies that inspired his work for years. Varley joined Cotman's Sketching Society. In 1804 he helped to found the Old Watercolour Society. Varley's own pupils included for a time John Linnell, David Cox and Peter de Wint. He published several treatises on composition. In person Varley was 'bull-like in strength and figure', a keen pugilist, and 'a man of the most generous impulses'. He believed fervently in astrology and visions, through which he became an artistic colleague of William Blake, whose sketch of him is reproduced here.

CORNELIUS VARLEY (1781-1873) joined his brother John on excursions to Wales in 1801 and 1803. His watercolours are now valued for their detailed observation and fresh-ness. Cornelius was an inventor and maker of scientific instruments – sundials, lenses, microscopes. His 'graphic telescope' was designed to enable artists to project images of a scene onto paper.

JOHN SELL COTMAN (1782-1842), born in Norwich, went to London as assistant to Rudolf Ackermann, engraver, of the Strand. He was welcomed by Dr Thomas Monro's circle of artists who met in Adelphi Terrace. In 1800 and 1802 Cotman toured Wales, an inspiration for his art. He became a leading member of the Sketching Society. In 1806 Cotman returned to

Norwich and took pupils, for whom he established a collection of 600 draw-ings that might be copied. In 1811 he succeeded 'Old Crome' as President of the Norwich Society of Artists. He etched many architectural subjects and produced several books. Cotman married a Norfolk-born wife, and had a family. In 1834 he returned to London, to the post of Drawing Master at King's College.

GEORGE ROBERT LEWIS (1782-1871) was born in London. He studied at the RA Schools. In 1813 Lewis went to Wales with John Linnell to paint in the open air. Religious, Linnell and he lived on a 'semi-Mosaic' diet. He painted 'on the spot' his Herefordshire harvest scenes from Haywood Lodge, and elsewhere sketched farmworkers, their tools and their carts. He returned to engraving and travelled in France and Germany. Phrenology was a passion; Lewis chose his wife in 1823 because of the pleasing shape of her head, and he published *Illustrations of Phrenology* (1841). Lewis retained interest in Herefordshire; he published *Illustrations of Kilpeck Church* (1842); *The Ancient Church of Shobden* [sic], *Herefordshire* (1852) and *An address on the subject of education* (1838), printed in Hereford. Lewis exhibited portraits and landscapes at the RA and elsewhere from 1820 to 1859.

DAVID COX (1783-1859), born in Birmingham, was a pupil of Joseph Barber and became a screen-painter for Birmingham's Theatre Royal. He transferred to London in 1804. Cox toured Wales with Charles Barber, Joseph's son, and there first painted in watercolour. He exhibited with

the Old Water Colour Society. John Varley recommended pupils to Cox; for them Cox published influential drawing books. He married Mary Agg, his landlady's daughter. From 1814 to 1826 Cox was in Hereford, until 1819 as drawing-master in Miss Croucher's School for Young Ladies in Widemarsh Street. He had private pupils too, Joseph Ince among them. Cox learned from Uvedale Price to admire the picturesque in landscape. He and Mary returned to London. In 1841 they moved to Harborne village near Birmingham. Each year with other artists they visited Betws-y-Coed.

EDMUND WARD GILL (1794-1854), father of E.M. Gill, was a painter of portraits and of 'The Hereford Cow'. He exhibited at the RA and the British Institution, then moved in 1823 from London to Ludlow. In 1826 he resided in Bye Street (now Commercial Street) Hereford. He lived in both Leominster and Ludlow for a time, and twice returned to Hereford, where in the 1840s the whole of the artistic family was reunited.

EDMUND MARINER GILL (1820-94). Reared in Hereford, 'Waterfall Gill' was a student under Mr Thornecraft of Ludlow and painted in the valley of the Teme. Charles Phillips, barrister of Hereford, purchased many of his pictures and recommended him to others. With an introduction to David Cox he went to London, and was admitted in 1843 to the Royal Academy Schools. Gill travelled through Scotland, Wales and the mountainous parts of England to paint, most famously, waterfalls and rapids in rivers. He exhibited in the Royal Academy between 1842 and 1886 and 'lived variously in London, Ludlow and Hereford'.

WILLIAM WARD GILL (1823-1894), painter of Hereford from Venns Lane, was the second son of E.W. Gill. He lived in Ludlow and Hereford. As a landscape painter, his studies of foliage were admired. Initially a watercolourist, he used oils after 1841, when he exhibited pictures at Liverpool. He travelled in the Lake District, north Wales and Scotland.

JACOB GEORGE STRUTT (1784-1867), from Colchester, studied in London, painted portraits and forest scenery, and between 1824 and 1826 exhibited at the RA. He married in 1813 Elizabeth Byron, author of virtuous romances. As 'Mrs Strutt' she wrote *Genevieve* (1818), *Chances and Changes* (1835) and guides for female travellers to France, Italy and Switzerland. Jacob Strutt is best known for two books of engravings, *Sylva Britannica, or, Portraits of forest trees, distinguished for their antiquity, magnitude, or beauty* (1822, expanded 1830) and *Deliciae silvarum* (1828). In 1831 the Strutts went to Lausanne. They then settled in Rome, where Jacob shared a studio with his second son. In the RA he exhibited 'Tasso's Oak, Rome' (1851) and other views of the campagna.

CHARLES FORDE WALKER (1803-57). In three years, 1849-1851, Walker painted in watercolour 300 churches in the Hereford diocese. Hereford City Library now holds the album containing these paintings. Walker, one deduces, had been commissioned by Bishop Hampden to depict the churches of his new see. Little is known of Walker. He was born in Greenwich, by 1851 he was an artist in Ludlow, and there he died. His delightful sketches often capture the aspect of the churches before they were 'improved' by Victorian architects. A hundred of Walker's sketches are reproduced in *Hereford*

Churches through Victorian Eyes ed. J. Leonard (Logaston Press, 2006).

JOHN SCARLETT DAVIS (1804-45) was the son of a watchmaker of Leominster. His friend from childhood was Joseph Ince from Presteigne, both gifted young artists. Davis, like Ince, may have taken lessons in Hereford with David Cox. Davis boarded at art school in Hackney then went to the Royal Academy Schools. In 1822 he exhibited in the Academy. Davis sketched in Wales, was admired as a portraitist, lived for three years in Yorkshire, and became known for perspective interior views of galleries, churches and palaces. He married and had three children. The family travelled with him in Europe; he painted in Paris, Venice, Antwerp, the Louvre and the Uffizi. John Hinxman, a merchant, funded their travels and came to own 489 of Davis' works. Davis died aged 41 of tuberculosis.

SAMUEL PALMER (1805-81) exhibited at the Royal Academy at the age of 14. John Linnell introduced him to William Blake. Between 1822 and 1835 Palmer lived in Shoreham in Kent, where gathered 'The Ancients', Blake-influenced artists, amongst them George Richmond and Edward Calvert. In Shoreham Palmer produced his great works – pastoral landscapes, demi-paradises, mysterious, visionary, often beneath a crescent moon. He married Hannah, Linnell's young daughter, and they moved to Marylebone. Palmer's paintings became more conventional and he taught drawing. Later, to Milton's poems and to his own translation of Virgil, he etched illustrations in which he recaptured his former vision of nature's mystery. In 1862 Palmer, Hannah and their children moved to Redhill in Surrey.

JOSEPH MURRAY INCE (1806-59) was born in London, his mother of French aristocratic birth, his father a doctor who became a GP in Presteigne. They lived in Broad Street. Joseph's friend, John Scarlett Davis, shared a passion for fishing and equalled his artistic talent. Ince studied under David Cox. On moving to London (1826) he exhibited at the RA and with the Society of British Artists. He used either oil or watercolour in seascapes, in views of Stockholm, and in scenes of Herefordshire and Radnorshire. He drew the old college buildings of Cambridge. Ince married in 1834 Sarah Phillips of Presteigne. They sketched in Devon, and Cambridge. The following summer in childbirth Sarah died. After that, Ince moved between Presteigne and London. He visited Oxford (1836), Wales (1839-40) and Cambridge, where, in the 1850s, he lived in King's Parade.

SIDNEY RICHARD PERCY, born Sidney Richard Percy Williams in 1821 in London, was a member of the Williams family of painters, who were related to such famous artists as James Ward and George Morland. His father, Edward Williams, a well-known landscape artist, taught him how to paint; otherwise he received no formal instruction. His early paintings were signed 'Sidney Williams'; he used the name 'Percy' to differentiate himself from the other artists in his family. Starting in 1842, he exhibited at the Royal

Academy, the British Institution, and the Suffolk Street Gallery of the Society of British Artists.

 JOHN EVERETT (1876-1949), born in Dorchester, attended the Slade and, briefly, the Académie Julian. In 1898 he joined as 2nd mate the *Iquique*, sailing to Sydney. He then returned to café society in London, and to painting in France and Cornwall. He married a fellow Slade student, his cousin Katherine. They honeymooned on a 700-ton barque to Australia – not happily – then lived in Dorset with their two sons. The marriage failed. Everett joined the merchant navy. During the 1920s and 1930s he chose to sail on a major voyage each year, drawing or painting shipboard scenes and waves. He left to the Maritime Museum a thousand of his seascapes. Everett's 'Monnington on Wye' is unusual, being distant from his homeland and the sea.

 BRIAN HATTON (1887-1916) was born in Hereford. His father was in the leather trade. In 1895 the family moved to Broomy Hill, Breinton. Considered frail, Brian was schooled in the sea air of Swansea. He drew and painted precociously – horses, carts, farming scenes, the landscape of Warham, the water-meadows of the Lugg, and portraits of sisters Ailsa and Marjorie. G.F. Watts, the doyen of painters, believed Hatton would become the greatest artist of his generation. Hatton spent two terms at Trinity College, Oxford; he then transferred to Arbroath's Hospitalfield Art College. He joined Petrie Flinders' archaeological expedition (1908), and attended the Académie Julian in Paris. Brian married Lydia May

Bidmead from Hereford, a teacher of dancing. Daughter Mary Amelia was born in 1915, just before Brian's posting to Egypt. In the Sinai he rode by mischance into a Turkish detachment, and died on Easter Monday 1916. A thousand of Hatton's works – watercolours, oils drawings, prints – are cherished, through his widow's generosity, by Hereford City Art Gallery.

 GILBERT SPENCER (1892-1976), born at Cookham, followed artist brother Stanley to the Slade. His studies were interrupted by war-service in Macedonia in the Medical Corps. In 1919 he was invited back to the Slade with a scholarship. In the 1920s he met Lady Ottoline Morrel who was pleased to give him accommodation in Garsington, so he came to enjoy the company of the 'Bloomsbury set'. Influenced by Stanley he produced 'Crucifixion' and 'Shepherds Amazed'. Subsequently he was a landscape painter, admired for the clarity of his colour, and a painter of murals – in Holywell Manor, in the student's union of University College, London, and in the Royal Academy restaurant.

 DAVID JONES (1895-1974) painted portraits, landscapes, and Arthurian and religious subjects; he engraved in wood and designed painted inscriptions. Jones attended Camberwell Art School, then soldiered on the Western Front – at Mametz Wood and Ypres. He interwove the horrors of the trenches with Shakespearean reference and Welsh mythology in an epic poem, *In Parenthesis* (1937), hailed by T.S. Eliot as 'a work of genius'. Jones became a Catholic in 1922, joined Eric Gill's Guild in Sussex, and from 1924 to 1927

visited Gill at Capel-y-ffin. Jones suffered nervous breakdowns in 1933 and 1947, woeful happenings which seemed to release his creativity. *Anathemata*, another long poem, was published in 1952; *Art and Sacrament*, a call for Catholic craft and culture, in 1955. Jones was made a Companion of Honour in 1974.

Edgar Holloway (1914-2008) of Mexbor-ough near Doncaster, left school at 14. He etched and printed with little tuition. At 17 he was invited to join the Society of Artist Printers in Edinburgh. Three years later his exhibition in London included a portrait of T.S. Eliot. Holloway converted to Catholicism (1941), inspired by Eric Gill. In Capel-y-ffin, where Gill had lived in the 1920s, he met Daisy Monica Hawkins, who had been Gill's model. Within six weeks they married. They lived by the Honddu until 1949 when they joined the Guild of St Joseph and St Dominic in Ditchling in Sussex. For twenty-two years Holloway was a graphic designer. Late he returned to landscape drawing – of the South Downs, Wales, Spain and France – and to etching. His series of thirty-three etched self-portraits are, like Rembrandt's, tough and moving records of youth and aging.

Trevor Makinson (1926-92) was born in Southport, Lancashire. A student at Hereford College of Art, he exhibited with Hereford Arts and Crafts and Wye Valley Arts Society. Subsequently he went to the Slade and taught at Glasgow School of Art and at the university. He exhibited regularly at the Royal Academy and the Royal Scottish Academy.

Martin Griffiths. From childhood on a small farm in Suckley on Herefordshire's borders, Martin attended Stourbridge and Wolverhampton Colleges of Art and established a ceramics studio in Cirencester. He has taught art and English, and has exhibited in Worcester and Birmingham Art Galleries. He says, 'Landscape has always been a major part of my life, whether on the farm, in an art Gallery, or when returning home, walking back over the Birch-wood Hills, seeing the Herefordshire valley spreading out before me, and hearing Elgar in my head.'

Edward Kelly, from Liverpool, studied in Italy on a John Moore's Scholarship. He taught painting for 25 years at Chelsea College of Art. Edward's home for three decades has been in the Wye valley, the beauty of which he has been keen to preserve. He was a founder of the Campaign for Poly-tunnel Control, which achieved a success in the High Court. His 'St Dubricius polyptych' is in Madley Church, as is his triptych 'Lilies of the Field'. Edward's River Series of paintings was inspired by the River Wye, his Bull Series both by old Greek imagery and by his walks among cattle on river-pastures below his studio.

Vanessa Pomeroy trained in Fine Arts at the Universities of Newcastle and Bologna. She has lectured in sculpture, art and design and the history of art, and has exhibited in places including London, Italy and Herefordshire. The Black Mountains are an inspiration for her paintings, which explore the range's broad panoramas, changing atmosphere, colour and dramatic light. Other subjects include gardens and seascapes. She lives and works in Eaton Bishop.

ALLAN MACDOUGALL's paintings and photographs depict the landscapes of Herefordshire, Wales, the Highlands of Scotland and Europe. As a trained photographer, he has a keen sense of the fleeting effects of lighting, mood and atmosphere. Allan works as a counsellor and psychotherapist. He has always been captivated by the Herefordshire landscape and in 1996 decided to try watercolour painting. He has held exhibitions in Edinburgh, north Wales as well as at Hereford Art Week. Allan is a keen mountaineer. He seeks to capture the uniqueness of the mountainous areas he visits and finds Scotland and Wales particularly inspiring.

TIM ROSSITER, born in Bristol in 1952, left school without qualifications but later trained as a fine artist. In 1989 he moved to the Black Mountains. He worked on art schemes to improve the environment of psychiatric hospitals and became increasingly involved in community art schemes. In 2005 he was festival director of the Dragon Gateway Arts Festival.

LUKE PIPER (b.1966). His first major show was in 1992 at the CCA Dover Street gallery, which also featured work by his father Edward Piper and grandfather John Piper. After studying at Frome College, Somerset he went on to read geography at Cambridge University. His course amongst other things led him to Melanesia on an anthropological assignment to study tribal warfare. This interest in the human and physical aspects of our landscapes has remained with him throughout his painting career.

Publisher's acknowledgements

Paintings

Special thanks to Hereford's Museum Service for images of many works by Brian Hatton, as well as David Cox's *Butcher's Row, Hereford*; Joshua Cristall's *Herefordshire Lady*; *Foxley*, by Anthony Devis; John Everett's *Monnington-on-Wye*; Edmund Mariner Gill's *Mill in Ruins on the Bank of the River Usk*; Edmund Ward Gill's *Hereford Cow*; William Ward Gill's *Hereford from Venns Lane*; Godfrey Kneller's portrait of Robert Harley; *March in Herefordshire* by Trevor Makinson; Gilbert Spencer's works *Orchard at Tarrington* and *Tarrington Court*; and *Hereford, Wye Bridge and Cathedral* by C. Westwood. Thanks in particular to the museum's collections officer of fine and decorative art, Catherine Willson for her generous help and support. Thanks also to Herefordshire Libraries for permission to include the paintings of churches by Charles F. Walker, and to Malcolm Thurlby for the image of the Sheela na Gig at Kilpeck church.

Our grateful thanks also to the following museums and galleries:

Brecknock Museum, for *Brecon on the River Usk* by John Varley

The British Library for the manuscript of *Sumer is icumen in* (Harley MS 978 fl 1v) and Christopher Saxton's *Hand-coloured Map of Herefordshire, 1610*

The Fitzwilliam Museum, Cambridge, for Samuel Palmer's *Tintern Abbey from near the Chepstow Road, looking towards Monmouth* (© Fitzwilliam Museum, Cambridge)

The Haworth Art Gallery, Accrington, Lancashire for Joshua Cristall's *The Gleaners* (© Haworth Art Gallery, supplied by Bridgeman Images)

The Henry E. Huntington Library and Art Gallery, California, for the image of Rowland Vaughan's *The Commonwealth*

Monnow Valley Arts for the images of Edgar Holloway's works *Mountain Path*; *Capel-y-Ffin, towards Hay Bluff*; *Craswall*; and *Offa's Dyke, Bradnor*; and also *Landscape at Capel-y-Ffin* by David Jones

Llyfrgell Genedlaethol Cymru/The National Library of Wales for *Hay on Wye and the Brecon Beacons* by Joseph Murray Ince; and also for an image of David Jones's painting *Tir y Blaenau*

Norwich Castle Museum & Art Gallery for Nicholas Pocock's *Wye Tour Boat passing Welsh Newton* (sometimes listed as *Dixton Church near Monmouth on the Wye*)

The Tate Gallery for three works by Joshua Cristall (*Arcadian Landscape*; *Interior of a Stable*; *Monnow Bridge at Monmouth*), three works by George Robert Lewis (*Harvest Field with Reapers, Haywood, Herefordshire*; *Hereford, Dynedor and the Malvern Hills*; *Hereford from the Haywood, noon*); *Llanthony Abbey*, by John Sell Cotman; and John Varley's *View of Bodenham and the Malverns* (all © Tate Gallery, London)

The Victoria and Albert Museum for *The Market Place, Ross* by Cornelius Varley; *The River Teme at Downton* by Thomas Hearne; *Lugg Meadow near Hereford* by David Cox; and George Robert Lewis's sketch *Agricultural Workers*

The Whitworth Gallery, Manchester, for *Beech Trees at Foxley, Herefordshire, with Yazor Church in the Distance* by Thomas Gainsborough (image courtesy of the Whitworth Gallery © The University of Manchester)

The Yale Center for British Art for *Crickhowell, Breconshire* by J.S. Cotman; Samuel Palmer's *Tintern Abbey at Sunset*; *A Peasant Girl Shading her Eyes* by Joshua Cristall; and *Ryelands Sheep* by James Ward

Our thanks also to the Trustees of the Estate of David Jones for allowing us to include his paintings, and to the following individual artists for allowing us to include their work in this collection:

Martin Griffiths, for *Sunset, Bromyard to Hereford road*

Edward Kelly, for an angel from his *St Dubricius polyptych* in Madley Church, his painting *Moonlight* and for his stone platter, *Fish in Ross on Wye*

Allan Macdougall, for *Winter in the Olchon Valley*

Luke Piper, for *Whitney-on-Wye*

Vanessa Pomeroy, for *Spring Light, Yellow Field, Hay Bluff*

Tim Rossiter, for *Llanthony Abbey*

Poems

Our heartfelt thanks to the many people who have generously given us permission to include the work of many poets:

To Ruth Bidgood and her publisher, Seren Books, for their permission to include her poems 'Cwmioie', 'The Hedge', 'Resurrection Angels', 'Merthyr Clydawg', 'Olchon Valley', 'Patricio 2001' and 'Singing to Wolves, Llanthony'.

To Jim Dening for permission to include his poems 'Herefordshire Ways of Looking at a Barn' and 'In the Borderlands'.

To Edward Harley for permission to include the Harley Manuscript.

To Roger Garfitt, Frances Horovitz' literary executor, for permission to include her work; and to Glenn Storhaug of Five Seasons Press for her 'Rowlestone Haiku', and for 'Prayer to the Lady of Kilpeck', originally published in *The Kilpeck Anthology* (1981); also to Bloodaxe Books for permission to include 'Old Song' and 'Evening'.

To the literary estate of Ronald Johnson for permission to include selections from Ronald Johnson, *The Book of the Green Man*, © 1967, reprinted in the Uniformbooks edition, 2015.

To the Society of Authors for permission to include a section of John Masefield's 'The Everlasting Mercy'.

To Glyn Mathias for permission to include two poems by his father, Roland Mathias: 'Thomas ap Richard of Doier to the Tower, These' and 'Craswall'.

To Margot Miller for her poem 'Hole in the Wall'.

To the Barbara Levy Literary Agency for permission to include Siegfried Sassoon's poem 'At the Grave of Henry Vaughan'. The poem is copyright Siegfried Sassoon by kind permission of the Estate of George Sassoon.

To Anne Stevenson for giving her blessing to the project, and to her publisher Bloodaxe Books for permission to include 'Orcop', 'Walking Early by the Wye' and 'The Parson and the Romany'.

To Bonnie Thurston and her publisher Liturgical Press for her poem 'Sheela na Gig'. (© 2011 by Order of Saint Benedict. Published by Liturgical Press, Collegeville, Minnesota.) Her poem 'St Mary's Church, Craswall' first appeared in no. 20 of the short-lived *Cantilupe Journal*, copyright of the Dean and Chapter of Hereford Cathedral; thanks to the cathedral's librarian, Dr Rosemary Firmin, for her help with this.

We have made every effort to seek out the copyright holders of paintings and poems. Please let us know of any omissions, so that they can be rectified in any future edition.